Lethbridge College - Buchanan Library

Next-Generation
Wellness at Work

NEXT-GENERATION WELLNESS AT WORK

Stephenie Overman

PRAEGER
An Imprint of ABC-CLIO, LLC

A B C 〰 C L I O

Santa Barbara, California • Denver, Colorado • Oxford, England

Copyright 2009 by Stephenie Overman

All rights reserved. No part of this publication may be reproduced, stored in a retrieval system, or transmitted, in any form or by any means, electronic, mechanical, photocopying, recording, or otherwise, except for the inclusion of brief quotations in a review, without prior permission in writing from the publisher.

Library of Congress Cataloging-in-Publication Data

Overman, Stephenie.

  Next-generation wellness at work / Stephenie Overman.
    p. ; cm.
  Includes bibliographical references and index.
  ISBN 978-0-313-36029-9 (alk. paper) — ISBN 978-0-313-36030-5 (ebook)
  1. Employee health promotion.   2. Occupational health services.   I. Title.
  [DNLM: 1. Occupational Health.   2. Health Promotion.
  3. Organizational Innovation.   WA 400 O96n   2009]
    RC969.H43O94   2009
    658.3'82—dc22   2009030396

13   12   11   10   9   1   2   3   4   5

This book is also available on the World Wide Web as an eBook.
Visit www.abc-clio.com for details.

ABC-CLIO, LLC
130 Cremona Drive, P.O. Box 1911
Santa Barbara, California 93116-1911

This book is printed on acid-free paper ∞

Manufactured in the United States of America

Every reasonable effort has been made to trace the owners of copyright materials in this book, but in some instances this has proven impossible. The author and publisher will be glad to receive information leading to more complete acknowledgments in subsequent printings of the book and in the meantime extend their apologies for any omissions.

For my parents
John and Mary Lou Overman

Contents

Acknowledgments

Next-Generation Wellness at Work grew out of a long list of best practices at successful companies. That list, and the experience of company wellness management officials, contributed greatly to the book's conclusions. I thank all those who shared their time and expertise.

I would also like to thank my husband, Steve Taylor, for all his help and support.

Introduction:
Beyond the Water Bottle

Twenty years ago, company wellness programs were an add-on, a nice extra. Company representatives passed out water bottles in promotions that encouraged employees to eat healthy and get more exercise.

However, the link to health-care costs and productivity was tenuous, and when budgets needed to be cut, wellness initiatives were often the first to go.

We're long past the point where a wellness program can be a soft add-on. Health-care costs are too high. The loss of productivity is too great. Competition in this economic climate is too fierce.

The best wellness initiatives have moved far beyond the 20th-century feel-good programs. Today, wellness managers must—and can—measure the results of their programs, proving that they reduce costs and increase productivity. Return on value is the new necessity.

Fortunately, a well-crafted wellness program is as good for employers as it is for employees. In addition to cutting health-care costs and increasing productivity, it enhances the employer brand. A company with a respected brand is one that people want to work for, want to contribute to, and want to stay with.

There's a lot to learn from the best practices of companies that are doing wellness right. For *Next-Generation Wellness at Work,* I've interviewed many people who are justifiably proud of their programs. Their companies are winners of prestigious honors: the WELCOA Well Workplace Award, the C. Everett Koop National Health Award, the National Business Group on Health Best Employers for Healthy Lifestyles Award, and the American Psychological

Association Psychologically Healthy Workplace Award. (See Appendix A.)

These are companies to not only admire but to look to for ideas when building a wellness strategy of your own. Their examples can help you and others successfully make the move beyond the water bottle.

Chapter One

First, the Payoff

Wellness has moved up in the world.

Stock in wellness is rising, fueled by concerns about rising health costs and the realization by companies that having a healthy workforce not only benefits their workers but also their bottom lines.

There's been a shift from viewing wellness as a soft benefit, a feel-good benefit, to recognizing it as part of the organization's overall health-care strategy. Savvy organizations have come to realize that, effectively managed, a healthy workforce is a competitive advantage in a tough market. They've also come to realize that the payoff for their investment won't only be years down the road, but more immediately because a healthier workforce is a more productive one.

It's certainly no secret that for the past two decades spending on health insurance has significantly outpaced both workers' earnings and the rate of inflation. In 2009, companies were expected to spend, on average, $9,660 per employee for health benefits, an increase of 6 percent from 2008.[1]

If food prices had risen at the same rates as medical inflation since the 1930s, we would be paying $80.20 for a dozen eggs and $107.90 for a dozen oranges.[2]

Everyone is concerned about health-care costs, employee and employer alike. The Congressional Budget Office has gone so far as to call the rising costs of health care and health insurance "a serious threat to the future fiscal condition" of the United States.[3]

ABSENTEEISM AND PRESENTEEISM

In addition to ever-higher medical costs, employers must cope with the high cost of absent workers. Absenteeism is linked to as much as

36 percent of payroll, or more than twice the cost of health care.[4] The 300 largest employers in the United States estimated that unscheduled absenteeism costs their businesses, on average, more than $760,000 per year in direct payroll costs.[5]

The cost of absence can be far greater than just wage replacement payments for lost time. Dr. Thomas Parry, president of Integrated Benefits Institute in San Francisco, notes that a company also bears "the opportunity costs associated with how it manages those absences—additional staff to have workers in reserve, the use of overtime or temporary help; the impact on the work performance of other team members or revenue lost through production shortfalls."

Smart employers have learned to measure not just the cost of absenteeism but also the productivity cost of *presenteeism*—which occurs when an underperforming worker is present but distracted, for example, by physical or mental illness. Presenteeism accounts for 61 percent of an employee's total lost productivity and medical costs.[6]

But there is hope. The health-care costs of people with chronic diseases such as diabetes and cardiovascular disease account for more than 75 percent of the medical care costs in the United States.[7] That means that there's much that individuals, with the help of their employers, can do to bring these costs down by making healthy lifestyle changes.

HARD NUMBERS

Organizations are searching for proof that wellness programs can reduce health-related costs and help improve the bottom line. Academics, company wellness professionals, and consultants have compiled a wealth of proof.

Watson Wyatt's 2007 Staying @ Work Report has some impressive numbers to offer: employers with the most effective health management programs achieved 20 percent more revenue per employee, had 16.1 percent higher market value, and delivered 57 percent higher shareholder returns.[8]

Dr. Dee W. Edington, director of the University of Michigan Health Management Research Center, has done extensive research on the effect of risk factors such as high cholesterol, obesity, and tobacco use on health costs. He finds that costs increase as the number of dangerous risk combinations increases. "However, wellness interventions designed to shift a high-risk individual into a lower-risk category can save as much as $4,078 in annual costs," notes Edington. The earlier people engage in changing their health status, the sooner risks are minimized and health-care costs are reduced, according to Edington. His research also shows that employee productivity decreases as health risks increase.[9]

Larry Chapman, senior vice president of WebMD Health Services and a trustee of the National Wellness Institute, has conducted an evaluation of 56 peer-reviewed journal articles on worksite health-promotion programs. Chapman found such programs produced an average 26.1 percent reduction in health costs, an average 26.8 percent reduction in sick-leave absenteeism, and an average 32 percent reduction in workers' compensation and disability management claims costs. He also measured an average $5.81 savings for every dollar invested.

Return on investment (ROI) is a key measure in the business world. In the wellness world, ROI is usually measured by determining the ratio of medical expenses not incurred to the total costs of wellness, including incentives paid to employees to participate. One commonly cited ROI range is 1.5:1 to 3:1 after three to five years, meaning that for every dollar invested in wellness, employers saved or can expect to save between $1.50 and $3.[10]

Experts warn against dazzling ROI claims that purport to show many dollars saved in a short period of time, but they say a well-designed, well-implemented program can positively affect health-care and health-related costs. One analyst says that while in the first year you should expect a net investment rather than a return, it's possible to start seeing a return on your investment in the second year and more likely in three to five years.

A 3-to-1 return specifically on health-care costs is the rule of thumb, but that doesn't look at other productivity factors that are estimated to be 3 to 10 times the direct medical costs. Even taking the conservative estimate, it's a significant return, according to one prominent analyst, David Anderson, senior vice president and chief health officer of StayWell Health Management, St. Paul, Minnesota.

The Health Project, a private-public organization formed to bring about behavioral changes in the American health-care system, carefully tracks the success of its C. Everett Koop Award winners:

- For every dollar Motorola invested in wellness benefits, the company saved $3.93. In 2000, that meant a $6,479,673 savings in the

United States. The company and employees saved approximately $6.5 million a year for lifestyle-related diagnoses such as obesity, hypertension, and stress.

- The Pepsi Bottling Group reported a return on investment of $1.70 for every dollar spent. Annual medical savings were estimated as averaging $264 per participant.
- USAA reported that workplace absences have decreased, with an estimated three-year savings of more than $105 million.
- The UAW-GM LifeSteps Health Promotion Program reported medical savings of $97 per participant per year and a disability/absence savings of $240 per participant per year.

ROI MODELS

It's often difficult to measure the ROI of a wellness program, but several nonprofit organizations are offering models to help you get started. Wellness Council of America (WELCOA) offers a free ROI calculator at Wellsteps.com. To use WELCOA's calculator, you'll need your company's total health-care costs over the past year, the total number of employees receiving benefits, and the percentage change in health-care costs per year for the past five years.

The calculator can show the cost of doing nothing—what will happen to your health-care costs over the next few years if you make no changes, based on health-care cost increases continuing as they have. Second, the calculator can project about how much money you could save if you decreased the percentage of workers who smoke or who are obese. Finally, the calculator can project what you would save on employee costs after implementing a low-, medium-, or high-intensity wellness program, according to WELCOA.[11]

The Alliance for Wellness ROI Inc., which is working to standardize wellness programs so that return on investment can be objectively measured, is launching an "ROI Valuation modeler" that will be able to calculate an estimated ROI for your company's wellness program, including individual components as well as aggregate program costs, compared to other companies.

The Corporate Executive Board also offers tools to estimate the returns you can expect from wellness, according to Michal Kisilevitz, who leads The Corporate Executive Board's benefits roundtable. "You used to be able to get away with 'Trust me. It will have an impact,'" she says. "But now a lot of our members feel that pressure to demonstrate returns. They hear, 'Make the case and convince me.'" It's initially difficult to show the value of wellness, she adds, because "if you do it well you are avoiding cost, not reducing costs. But over time you will see a reduction in cost because you won't have as many people sick."

Mary Liz Murphy, head of LifeForce Solutions Inc., sees a shift from measuring ROI to measuring "value on investment." It's a more meaningful measurement, according to Murphy, who is also project leader for the Conference Board's research working group "The Wellness Advantage." "Value on investment looks not only at financial indicators but also at participation indicators, screening indicators such as getting mammograms, health-risk indicators, clinical indicators, and utilization indicators," she says.

It's more challenging to add productivity indicators and shareholder value indicators, Murphy says, but researchers are in the "frontier stages" of research in those areas. With all of these indicators, you can better assess if what you're doing is working or not, she says, and if you are meeting the expectations of the different stakeholders—the CEO, the COO, shareholders, employees.

THE BOTTOM LINE

Health-care insurance isn't likely to get cheaper. Productivity isn't going to become any less important in this competitive climate. But the experience of workplace experts and a review of literature that examines the business rationale for worksite health promotion shows that when properly designed, a wellness program can increase employees' health and productivity.[12]

Now is the time to look at the numbers, to look at the potential payoff, and to implement a well-thought-out wellness strategy that truly benefits the bottom line. To execute that successful wellness strategy you'll need a champion at the top. Chapter 2 tells how to get senior-management buy-in.

Profile: Union Pacific Tracks Wellness Results (http://www.up.com)

Union Pacific Corporation sees a substantial payoff for its wellness initiative because it identifies its workers' most serious health risks, designs effective programs to reduce those risks, and tracks the results of its efforts.

Barb Schaefer, senior vice president, human resources, is adamant that "healthier employees who make good, informed decisions about their medical care help hold down rising health-care costs."[13]

Her motto is "An ounce of prevention is worth a pound of cure," because working on the railroad can be physically demanding for the mostly older workforce, some of whom are on call 24 hours a day. Fatigue is a chronic hazard. The prevention has plenty of time to pay off—the average employee stays more than 30 years with the company.

And Union Pacific has had plenty of time to hone its wellness initiative; it started the program back in 1987. Today, the "HealthTrack" program has four main components: employee assessment, analysis of the assessment results, targeted interventions, and periodic follow-ups. After evaluating the data, the Union Pacific health-promotion program seeks to raise awareness and control 10 targeted risk factors: alcohol consumption, blood glucose, blood pressure, cholesterol, nutrition, fitness, mental health, tobacco use, stress, and weight.

Over the years, Union Pacific has earned many honors for its efforts, including the WELCOA Well Workplace Platinum Award. WELCOA praises Union Pacific for "the most sophisticated approach available for supporting employee behavior change and affecting positive health and productivity outcomes. Instead of shooting from the hip, blindly hoping to help their population, UP uses assessment to develop the specific goals for Health Track. After gathering and evaluating this information, they are poised to implement targeted interventions designed to effectively reduce risk factors."[14]

The results, according to WELCOA, include the following:

- Blood pressure interventions have yielded a ratio of $4.29 saved for every $1 spent.
- Cholesterol interventions have yielded a ratio of $5.25 to $1.
- Smoking cessation interventions have yielded a ratio of $2.24 to $1.

The net effect of these interventions has been a cost ratio of $3.24 to every $1 invested, WELCOA notes, which is "highly significant when you consider that prior claims analyses have revealed that unhealthy behaviors cost approximately 40 million dollars per year during the 1990s."[15]

LINKING SAFETY AND HEALTH

Union Pacific coordinates safety, productivity, and health-care costs, says Jackie Austad, general director of health promotion and wellness, because "studies correlate health risks with safety. If you can improve health risks, the probability of injury goes down."

These studies show that stress, depression, fatigue, obesity, diabetes, and high blood pressure "significantly increase the likelihood of injury," she says. "We're trying to decrease the number of health risks, so we're confident we will get a corresponding decrease in costs. The goal is to make people healthier, to get that improvement to the bottom line."

The biggest challenge at Union Pacific now is weight, according to Austad. "It's the biggest health risk, and it impacts so many other health risks, such as cholesterol, blood pressure and diabetes. If we can improve weight, we can improve health in general."

To win the battle against the bulge, the company has given employees free access to more than 525 fitness centers system-wide, as well as a fitness facility at headquarters in Omaha, Nebraska. The Union Pacific Center also houses a dining room that features healthy cuisine. The company is proud to point out that 25 percent of sales are generated through the salad bar offerings. Even the vending machines offer healthy snack alternatives.

As the largest railroad in North America, Union Pacific has a lot of ground to cover to make sure its health message is communicated to its 50,000 employees in 23 states. A network of on-site regional health coordinators and occupational health nurses conduct health screenings and health fairs.

The unions are committed to improving employee health, says Austad. So is senior management. Union Pacific declared health and welfare one of its eight "Big Financial Deals" for the years 2001–2006, putting health on the same level as fuel costs and business in Mexico. Everyone wants "employees going home in as good or better shape than they came to work," she says.

Chapter Two

Start at the Top

Wellness starts at the top. If top management is not onboard, it's unlikely your wellness program can succeed. So you must be prepared to convince the C-suite that aligning wellness with the business strategy really does pay off.

That may be hard. Too often, wellness still has a soft or fluffy feel to it among C-suite folks who remember a first generation of wellness programs that didn't deliver genuine bottom-line benefits.

Times have changed. It's now time for senior executives to realize that far from being a light-weight option, wellness can be a solid business tool. It's not just something the organization does lightly, as a lagniappe, a small, extra gift, for its workers.

Top managers need to see employee health and well-being as part of the overall mission and understand that human capital needs to be invested in and maintained. If a piece of machinery does not function properly, the company knows it will lose money. Isn't it at least as important for people to function well?

Senior executives are the ones who must lead their company to the next level of health and productivity. They must make it a personal commitment. They must be the role models. It's going to be your job to convince them to step up to the task. What's the best approach to take? Top executives especially want to see the numbers. They want solid evidence that shows by spending money now they will save significant money in the medium and long term. As in other areas of business, they want to be sure they are getting the most bang for their buck.

Show your top management team that health improvements and cost savings are achievable by providing well-aimed, cost-effective wellness initiatives that reduce the risk factors that are often the root cause of costly diseases. Show them that wellness will deliver plenty of bang for their buck.

BUILDING THE CASE

To build a case for wellness, first interview members of upper management to find out their priorities. The wellness program will be run by the people on the floor, but the resources will be provided by upper management, so tailor your message to the needs of management.

Know your organization's priorities. Look at its credo, mission statement, and strategic business objectives to inform you about your company's priorities. If you can tie in your wellness program's objectives with your company's strategic business objectives, you'll stand a much better chance of success. A wellness program is a way of expressing the company's core values, because it is the top management's way of showing that the company is willing to deploy resources to keep employees healthy.

Know your organization's needs. If your organization is in the midst of a culture change, highlight how the wellness program can help smooth that process. If the company's profit margin is narrow, emphasize studies demonstrating a high dollar return for wellness programs. If the company is experiencing trouble in recruiting and keeping trained professionals, emphasize the impact of quality-of-life programs on morale, recruitment, and retention.

Demonstrate the real relationship between certain chronic illnesses and expenses. The categories that tend to be most expensive are heart disease, muscular/skeletal disorders, mental health, and some types of cancer. Lay out the information for management and show how lifestyle choices such as overeating and lack of exercise can contribute to these diseases.

"Look at the dollars spent. Look at absence, accident rates, workers compensation claims and, if you have it, productivity loss," suggests Dr. Ron Z. Goetzel, who is director of Emory University's Institute for Health and Productivity Studies, and a vice president for Thomson Reuters.

The next step is to convince senior management that you can actually do something about high-ticket conditions by showing them examples of evidence-based programs that have been demonstrated to work in other settings. Construct an ROI model, Goetzel says, "An econometric model that shows for every percentage drop in something like the obesity rate or hypertension, what that might [save] if you project forward. That's something the finance people can look at. It's like putting in new machinery—when do we expect to see savings, what will those savings be?" Make sure you distinguish these programs from the poorly designed ones they've certainly heard about where someone just hands out a flier that says "have a healthy lifestyle," and does nothing else.

SHOW THEM THE VALUE

A common obstacle is that human resource managers and wellness professionals often don't speak top management's language and understand their priorities. They don't know how to articulate the value that the business is getting for the money it spends on wellness.

Companies tend to look for return on investment, but with wellness programs, value on investment (VOI) is the big thing. "VOI means more than just lowering overall health care claims costs. It means actually gaining productivity," says Mary Liz Murphy, head of LifeForce Solutions Inc.

The cost of medical care is where most HR people put their time, but that covers only about 25 percent of total health-related costs, says Murphy, who also is project leader for the Conference Board's research working group, The Wellness Advantage.

When looking at wellness, the focus tends to be solely on medical expenditures, but a number of studies indicate that productivity loss is two to four times larger than medical expenditures. Companies aren't paying enough attention to the hidden costs of avoidable sick days and what is known as *presenteeism*—defined as the cost of employees who are on the job but not fully functioning due to medical conditions. These conditions may represent fewer *direct* costs than high-profile, high-expense diseases, such as cancer and heart disease, but they represent higher indirect costs because they are so prevalent.[1]

Working with MGM Mirage in Las Vegas on how wellness can improve productivity, Dr. Tom Parry focuses the discussion on the subject of shareholder value. "We're doing an economic analysis of the opportunity costs of lost time. We made the business case and got [senior management] buy in. We're just beginning to measure results," says Parry, president of Integrated Benefits Institute.

More and more, top management is willing to listen to the case for wellness. "As long as health-care costs were increasing at the rate of inflation, they didn't pay attention. When it went up, they noticed. We're finding great interest in the work we're doing, given the pressures that are driving medical costs, and a more and more competitive marketplace," Parry says.

So the advice is: get into the mind of CFOs. They have the fiduciary responsibility. Their job is to manage the risk and minimize the risk. Help them decide that assigning money to your program is going to give more value. CFOs particularly want to see the hard-dollar savings. They understand that these savings aren't likely to come in the first year, but within the next year, they want two dollars saved for every one dollar spent.

When you've got the numbers, tell the CFO. But when you've got the stories, tell the chief executive officer.

What's most effective with CEOs is not showing them a lot of data, but rather anecdotal information. It's giving them examples such as "remember the guy on the third shift who dropped dead of a heart attack?" It's underlining the fact that when a human life lost, it is also a loss to the company.

More often than not, says Larry Hicks, a senior consultant with the Hay Group, "that personal familiarity with someone's catastrophic illness is what leads CEOs to make decisions in favor of wellness initiatives."

Also sell the wellness program to the people you know the CEO listens to. Give them an opportunity to understand the economic return of wellness so that they can then make the best presentation to top management.

Another way to get senior executives' attention is to point out what the competition is doing. CEOs are very busy, and even if they are interested, wellness is just one of so many things on their dance card. But, there are competitive instincts that can help drive their involvement. "They benchmark against each other. When I was with an oil company, the executives would say 'tell me what the other major oil companies do,'" says Garry Lindsay, senior fellow and senior program officer for Partnership for Prevention's Leading by Example.

Leading by Example is a CEO-to-CEO initiative that focuses on the importance and value of worksite health promotion. Participating CEOs lead by example by making health promotion and disease prevention a part of their business strategy. When first building Leading by Example's membership, Lindsay found that the essential ingredient to participation was telling executives which other CEOs were involved, particularly within their own industry. "Once we got one supermarket chain, then other chains wanted to be involved," says Lindsay.

Connect your CEO with other CEOs who've already gotten the message. There's a concept known as *elephant bumping* and, according to Dr. David Hunnicutt, president of WELCOA, it can be powerful. CEOs get to the top because they are willing to work very hard and put up with a lot of things that other people aren't willing to tolerate, he says. "As a result of learning from the school of hard knocks, CEOs know things that other people don't. And that's why CEOs love to talk with other CEOs. Not only is it good for their egos, it's a great opportunity for them to rub shoulders with other apex predators that have followed the same path as themselves," says Hunnicutt.[2]

If there is a wellness industry standard for your particular industry, emphasize how the company's wellness program could actually surpass the industry standard and gain local, regional, or national recognition for the CEO and the business. As Kathy Cash, author of *How to Add Sparkle and Pizzazz to Your Health Promotion Program*, points out: "Senior management loves positive publicity."

A TASTE OF THEIR OWN MEDICINE

One of the reasons a wellness program never becomes a real part of the corporate culture is that senior level executives don't truly buy into the concept that healthier lifestyle choices equal better bottom-line results. To help your CEO see the light, consider enrolling him or her in an executive health program that is designed specifically to give company leaders a detailed snapshot of their personal health status. Executive health programs offer comprehensive executive physicals, with longer-than-usual doctor-patient consultations. These premium programs may even include such things as lifestyle counseling, personal fitness training, and massage.

There's no doubt these top-of-the-line programs can be expensive. Just the basic program can cost from $1,900 to $2,500. But you may be able to work out a deal with a local hospital for a less extravagant version.

The main component of any executive health program is the comprehensive physical. The physical includes a detailed medical history and a series of diagnostic tests such as screenings for diabetes and anemia, thyroid disease, and liver and kidney disease. There's also likely to be a lipid panel to assess cardiac and stroke risk factors, an electrocardiogram, a chest X-ray, and pulmonary-function test to assess lung problems. Once baseline data are established on the first visit, annual repeat visits are less comprehensive.

Beyond the comprehensive physical—and perhaps even more important—is the time that the executive health program allows the client for an in-depth consultation with the physician. At a time when health care is often severely limited by overscheduled physicians, the chance to spend a focused hour or more discussing test results and physical concerns is a luxury—and a selling point of most programs.[3]

An executive health program is not only a way to bring your senior executive into the wellness fold, it's a health assurance program that protects key assets. Executive health programs can save a company millions of dollars, according to a study of Bank One executives by the *Journal of Occupational and Environmental Medicine*. When Bank One compared health expenditures and productivity for executives who used the program with those who didn't, it found that participants' claims were 20 percent less than those of nonparticipants. It also found that participants' average number of workdays lost was 45 percent less. As a result, the bank estimated it saved $1,661 per executive over a three-year period. The savings seem to come more as a result of the time spent with the doctor and health specialists than from technology.[4]

MODELS AND CHAMPIONS

Once you've convinced top management that wellness is worth it, it's time for them to promote it, model it, and champion it. Have them communicate how wellness fits into the business objective. Encourage managers to support it because the philosophy needs to filter down to middle managers. Senior executives should send out a healthy company culture message by making sure their workers have opportunities to exercise, reduce stress, eat right, and stop smoking.

Send out a letter from the CEO that lays out the need for the well-ness program and the benefits it offers both employer and employ-ees (see Appendix B.) The letter should explain to employees how the cost of providing health benefits continues to rise and how instead of just shifting costs to employees, the organization is in a position of cost sharing. Make it clear that reducing health costs requires a partnership.

To make that partnership work, senior management needs to par-ticipate, to show that they're not just preaching but showing by example. For example, the CEO of one company made a video that showed him running on a treadmill. At another company, manag-ers led the 5K walk/run. And at Trek Bicycle Corp. in Waterloo, Wisconsin, the CEO started riding his bike to work.

Mike Campbell of the Wellness Council of Indiana recalls going out to breakfast with a bank president and owner who was inter-ested in starting a wellness program: "When I ordered, he said: 'Give me what he ordered.' He was getting the picture" that he needed to change his own behavior if he expected employees to change.

At another company Campbell cites, the CEO is a perfect role model because he works out, eats properly, and has personally been the driver behind changing the vending machines to healthier food. "This guy drives the benefits committee meetings. Wellness is the number one theme," says Campbell. That CEO's involvement has had a huge impact, according to Campbell, resulting in health-care costs that are far below the national trend.

At Quest Diagnostics Inc., based in Madison, New Jersey, two se-nior vice presidents staged a very public weight-loss competition. "We videotaped them in unflattering positions, and they gave their honest opinions about why they wanted to lose weight. They freely acknowledged their bad habits. It was done in a fun way, but it was useful," says Fred R. Williams, director of health management strat-egies for the diagnostics services provider. The vice presidents ex-changed e-mails with employees, asking for weight-loss tips and giving periodic updates on their progress. During the three-month weight-loss contest and the maintenance period that followed, both vice presidents did extraordinarily well.

The Chairman and CEO of Dow Chemical, Andrew Liveris, often spreads the word about wellness to other CEOs as well as to his own employees. As a spokesperson for the Leading by Example coalition, Liveris speaks to other executives about the importance of prevention as well as quality and patient safety efforts. He also has written about the importance of health in his personal blog on the corporate intranet site.

He has been a true champion for health at Dow, says Dr. Cathy Baase, global director of health services: "Mr. Liveris genuinely values people and life. He places health as a very high priority." But she adds that what first drew the Dow's CEO to the wellness cause was a thorough business analysis demonstrating the importance of health to business success.

At Dow, regional and business leaders include the topic of health in their leadership meetings, build health-related targets as components of their improvement plans, and communicate expectations to their staff. As a result, individual leaders around the company become champions for building the culture of wellness in their own way.

The company's experience points to a number of actions managers can take to be a force for success in developing and maintaining a healthy culture:

- Speak about health as a priority business issue with their staff
- Be an example by taking care of themselves
- Encourage members of their organization to participate in the health improvement activities and programs available to them
- Acknowledge that it is not always easy to be healthy and that everyone needs to provide active support to each other to be successful
- Be willing to share the story of their own healthy lifestyle struggles as appropriate in an effort to encourage others to take their health seriously

In all of this, sincerity matters. Never let top managers be hypocritical. Top management should realize that employees really notice if they say wellness is a priority but that they're not participating.

The Corporate Executive Board surveyed employees about actions consistent with stated wellness goals and found that about 70 percent think their bosses are not putting their money where their mouth is. What message does it send to employees, asks Michal Kisilevitz, "if you talk about having a smoking cessation program but you provide a nice area for smokers? Or you talk about healthy eating but you have doughnuts and other unhealthy food at a company meeting? Are you the one [holding] the meeting by walking around the building with someone [for exercise]? Or by having a smoking break with someone?"

It's important that top management give the right overall message with the actions they take, says Kisilevitz, who leads the Corporate Executive Board's benefits roundtable. Otherwise, there's more opportunity for doing harm than for improving health.

CARROTS FOR THE BOSS

Companies often give employees incentives for taking part in health initiatives (see chapter 5). Such carrots can work for managers and executives as well.

When Quest Diagnostics initiated its health assessment program, employees were not going to the health screenings, in part because their supervisors did not think it was important enough to give them the time off. So Quest established two sets of incentives—one for employees and another one for managers. Each business unit manager was required to have at least 50 percent participation in health assessments or the company would add a surcharge the next year that would add to the expense of the business unit, which would make it harder to show a profit. That, in turn, would affect profit sharing and managerial bonuses. Managers got the message, and participation rose to nearly 70 percent.

Companies in the manufacturing sector are particularly good at making use of such incentives. Often, "they have contests where [top managers] can earn a bonus by getting a certain participation level. It's not a large piece of the bonus, but it's large enough that they get people to participate," says Greg Lehman, president and CEO of the Minneapolis-based consulting firm HealthFitness. "It's not widespread but there are examples of where that's starting to catch on in the country," he says.

At 3M, each U.S. plant has an annual wellness goal; locations that successfully hit their targets earn a financial incentive. Each year, the 3M wellness team puts together what it wants plant managers at the various locations to do in support of their initiatives. Occupational health nurses and HR managers are the avenue to connect with employees at each plant. At the end of each year, if they meet their goals, they get about a $200 per employee rebate back to their operating budget. So far, compliance has been exceptional.

In the future, 3M plans to conduct health assessments and biometric screenings. Plant managers will be in charge of preparing their facilities for these wellness activities and for getting a certain percentage of their workforce to take part. If they hit their numbers, they will receive a rebate.

The company is promoting a more concerted wellness effort than it has had in the past. "We need to think in economic terms. We do a lot with negotiating with health-care insurers and clinics. Now we need to look at the demand side—keep [employees] healthy and to find appropriate care. We'll be better off from a cost standpoint," says Jack Arland, director of benefits.

In selling the program to top management, Arland emphasizes the long-term investment. "We have long-tenured employees. If we cover them for ten years and in retirement, it makes sense for us to have as healthy a population as possible."

KEY TO CULTURE CHANGE

Senior management support is the key that opens all doors, and such support can alter the very culture of your organization. When you have that kind of support, "you will have a way of getting change through to people. You will be able to work across the organization, weaving related efforts together" into an integrated wellness philosophy, says StayWell Health Management Senior Vice President and Chief Health Officer David Anderson. "Executives have big levers in terms of culture. This is a situation where they can really be the drivers. They are the number-one factor in whether a program is going to be successful," he says.

Over the years, Mike Campbell has seen many companies that have put together a wellness program that was stellar on paper but haven't been able to overcome a sick culture: "The culture is the conduit through which everything flows. If the conduit is rusty, what's coming through?"

Quest Diagnostics is focused on changing its culture to one of wellness, not just avoidance of illness. Williams says he knows that the change is complete "when I ask an employee 'What is your health plan?' and the person doesn't answer with the name of an insurance plan, but says, 'Well Fred, I walk this much, I try to eat right.'"

THE BOTTOM LINE

For your wellness program to succeed you've got to bring your CEO and your executive team onboard. To do that, show them the money. Build a case that demonstrates how an effective program can save on medical expenditures and insurance costs—and reap productivity gains as well. Show them how wellness can improve their own lives and how it can give your organization a competitive advantage over others in your field.

Once you've convinced top management that wellness is worth it, it's time for them to promote it, model it, and champion it. Have them communicate to employees how wellness fits into the business objective and improves their lives. Make sure executives walk that talk.

The next step is to form a wellness team or committee that can design and implement a well-thought-out program and handle employee feedback. Chapter 3 addresses these issues.

Profile: Cianbro's Healthy Family (http:www.cianbro.com)

Wellness is personal for Peter Vigue, president and CEO of Cianbro construction, an employee-owned company based in Pittsfield, Maine. He looks at the people he's responsible for as if they're his family and believes that, as such, "I should create the right atmosphere for them," an atmosphere that is tobacco free and a workplace where exercise and good nutrition are encouraged.

Vigue is adamant about wellness because he knows what it's like to lose a member of his extended family: "One of the folks at this company who I knew well had lung cancer. I had been involved with this person for many years, addressing other issues. I helped him work through alcohol-related issues and as a result he ended up being a real star player in our company. That came as result of my insistence that he get help, which we would provide, or leave the company. He made the right decision. He got help."

But the employee smoked and later died of lung cancer. "When that happened, it became clear that if I had taken a stronger position with smoking cessation, he might still be with us," Vigue says.

Rita Bubar, the company's corporate human resources director, knows how deeply the loss affected Vigue, and how much Vigue has affected Cianbro's wellness effects.

Bubar says Vigue is well aware that many valued employees are older and have some real life-threatening illnesses based on lifestyle-related causes. That concern is tied in with the frustration about how little the company can do about high medical costs. "We can't impact what doctors and hospitals charge. What is it that we *can* control? We can control our own personal behavior," Bubar says.

Cianbro works with Dr. Larry Catlett, its medical director and president of Occupational Medical Consulting. Instead of lecturing employees on healthy behavior, Catlett advocates *motivational interviewing*. Based on research by Stephen Rollnick and William R. Miller, motivational interviewing uses a client-centered approach that helps clients resolve their feelings of ambivalence about change and helps build the confidence required to change behavior.

Motivational interviewers develop listening skills that allow them to recognize issues about change that are important to the participant. "MI allows the participant to speak into an empathetic mirror. Important issues are then 'refracted'—that is, the positive side of change is stressed—back to the client to reinforce their motivation for change," according to Catlett.

For example, a health coach may have a client who expresses conflicting feelings about a behavior such as smoking. "The person might say 'I like the taste of smoking,' but 'I'll feel better about myself if I quit smoking' but 'I might gain weight if I quit.' The health coach then works with the person toward an acceptable resolution," Catlett explains.

The company views its wellness program as an extension of its safety program. "We're known as a leader in workplace safety and in preventing accidents. We have a behavioral based-safety program. We really just recognized that we could emulate our success with safety and create a total safety and wellness environment that shows that we care about people, not just at work. Wellness isn't just some separate program. Wellness is a part of our business strategy. It is tied to our strategic plan. We expect it really be run as a business program," say Bubar.

Perhaps one of the reasons Cianbro is so well regarded in the wellness field is because of the less traditional approaches it takes. Among its many honors, Cianbro is a WELCOA Platinum Award recipient.

The wellness program began with a successful six-month pilot program back in 1996. Over the next few years, Cianbro worked to take the pilot company-wide and in 2001 created the Healthy LifeStyle Program that is tied to the company's medical plan. Employees were told that they would pay more if they were not willing to help eliminate at-risk health behaviors. Since then the company has slowed its double-digit insurance increases to a single-digit increase.

In 2003 the company banned employee tobacco use, outdoors as well as indoors. A lot of companies are tobacco free, but probably not a lot who work in construction outside. "That caused quite a little stir in the industry. There was a little bit of a buzz that you can't do that in our environment. You'll lose people and won't be able to hire anybody. People will quit. None of that was true. We did an education period and put it in. There wasn't a ripple. Nobody quit. All the nonsmokers were 'hip, hip hurrah'," Bubar says.

To help employees quit smoking the company pays for all types of assistance, resulting in a 50 percent quit rate among those who enroll in some type of smoking cessation program. In 2005 the company extended the benefit to spouses.

The company understands that change is hard for people and works to create an environment where wellness is integrated into everything it does, where it is behavior based. It has to be a long-term program. "I don't believe that we can put short-term fixes into this," Bubar says.

Vigue also knows how difficult long-term change can be. He says he recently needed to have a heart-to-heart talk with senior managers who weren't continuing to set a good example. "So I got them in the room and talked about how they have to exercise every day. We got a trainer. They reported their dietary results daily. One gentleman has lost over a hundred pounds," Vigue says. "This is about leadership. I expect them to set the example or they're not going to be a leader any more."

"I do the same. I don't ask anybody to do anything I wouldn't do," he says. Vigue works out each day, alternating weight training and elliptical machine exercise. "Everybody has their own choice of how they exercise. We leave that up to them," he says.

If a company wellness program doesn't succeed, it's because top management is not engaged. "You can't delegate this. It has to start at the top," Vigue says. "You can't just do this to reduce health-care costs, but do it because you care about them. It's a moral responsibility. This is about walking the talk. It's not easy, but isn't that what leadership is all about?"

Chapter Three

Team Wellness

For wellness to work you'll need a team, or a committee or council, to set the overall strategy, work with senior management, get feedback from employees, and decide on the most effective initiatives.

Having some type of internal wellness advisory team is certainly a best practice if you're serious about having a healthier, more productive workforce. It's invaluable to bring representatives from all levels of the business together to help the organization better allocate time and resources and to set budgets and goals for your wellness effort.

You'll want your wellness committee to have its own mission statement, maybe even its own logo. It's smart to have an operating plan with an overall goal, a timeline, and what the Wellness Council of America likes to call SMART objectives: Specific, Measurable, Achievable, Realistic, and Time specific.[1] Your wellness team members should have a thorough understanding of the goals of the business and of how wellness fits into the overall business plan.

Team membership is a big job. Wellness programs aren't successful unless you get vigorous participation. "They have to be cheerleaders," is how Fiona Gathright, president of Wellness Corporate Solutions, describes it. The members should not only be enthusiastic, they should be willing to meet frequently and to stick to the agenda, says Gathright. Treat the wellness committee like any other committee. Have strong leadership and know what the goals are. Is the purpose to reduce health-care costs? To create a great place to work? To improve recruitment and retention goals?

There is no one-size-fits-all approach when it comes to putting together a wellness team. You'll want to customize your committee, depending upon the size of your company and the needs of your employees.

Is it best to appoint members of your wellness committee or to seek volunteers? Wellness pros come down on both sides of the question. From long experience as president of the Wellness Council of Indiana and employee benefits practice leader for Neace Luken, Mike Campbell finds that employers usually appoint committee members.

In that case, management should be careful to select team members who represent the various areas of the workforce and to select people who grasp how health and productivity complement the business goals. "They may have someone from the mail room, from administration, from the factory floor, depending on the nature of the business. At an Indianapolis law firm the committee includes a runner," an employee who delivers documents, Campbell says.

An advantage to an appointed team is that its members can concentrate on getting results, rather than spending time struggling for support from management.[2] But Joan Parks-Hubley says employees don't like to be "voluntold." She finds it best to "put out a general call to get people who are interested and motivated. That's better than having management select people." Hubley is coordinator of healthy workplaces for the Nova Scotia Public Service Commission. Every government department in the Canadian province has at least one healthy workplace committee, which includes representatives from other committees such as employee recognition and occupational and safety.

At Quest Diagnostics, a leading provider of diagnostic testing, being a committee member is a very visible volunteer position, done in addition to the individual's day job. But "it's not a heavy burden," according to Fred R. Williams, director of health management strategies. For example, the volunteer in charge of the smoking cessation program makes sure the program is explained to new employees during orientation. He or she also distributes posters, flyers, and other information and is the general go-to person for that part of the overall wellness program.

The Quest wellness committee represents each of the company's business units, with one person as wellness project manager. There are leaders within the committee for smoking cessation, fitness, health screenings, weight management, communications, and stress, with defined job descriptions for each role.

Ed Buffett believes being a wellness committee member should be clearly a volunteer role. But "just because people raise their hand and say they will do it isn't enough. You need to have an interview process. How committed are they? How much time will they give?" This interview enables an important dialogue to take place, says Buffett, president and CEO of Buffett & Company Worksite Wellness Inc. It not only gives the interviewer—the internal or external wellness professional—an opportunity to assess whether the employee is a person who is good at working in a team environment, but the interviewer gives the potential volunteer a good sense of the scope of the role.

STAKEHOLDERS AT THE TABLE

Companies structure their teams in different ways, depending on size, number of locations, resources, and culture. In all cases, the committee should be representative of the entire employee body.

For example, if it is a unionized environment, "you must have a representative from the union," Buffett says. "That's just as critical as having someone who is part of the management team. People are going to be looking at the various constituencies and ask 'is the union represented?' If not, there's the implication that the union is not an enthusiastic supporter. And if management does not have a representative on the committee, it's viewed as a sign that management is not taking this seriously." Every stakeholder needs a representative at the table, but Buffett says he frequently finds that isn't the case: "That's a mistake you see more oft times than you would think."

To head the committee, it's best if the chair is someone who is viewed by his or her peers as a leader, but not someone who is a part of top management. Employees should feel senior management supports, but doesn't control, the wellness initiative.

Fiona Gathright says her most successful clients do have wellness committees made up of employees from all levels of organizations. Senior management is represented, but they make sure to include members of the support staff as well. One client has been very successful because it has pulled together a team that represents the company from top to bottom, across divisions. They haven't given short shrift to the night shift. They time their meetings and initiatives to include them, she says. That's especially important because those night shift workers really need all the benefits a wellness program can provide. "Shift work puts an extra stress on your body," Gathright says.

WELCOA Platinum award winner Navistar International Corporation has 30 wellness teams throughout the company, each with 5 to 20 members. "These are volunteers who make trucks and engines for a living but who have a passion for health and wellness," says Dawn Weddle, wellness and behavioral health manager. With a global workforce of 18,000, Navistar also produces school buses, has a financing arm, and has the largest parts distribution network in the United States.

Navistar has had volunteer teams since the company started its wellness program more than 10 years ago. All sites have an annual operating plan, goals and objectives, marketing strategies, a timeline, and a budget. Each site has an executive sponsor, such as a high-level manager or vice president of HR, as well as a team leader who keeps the group on task.

All sites have job descriptions for team members, so when they come onto the team they know what to expect. Team members attend monthly meetings and are usually responsible for one or two events a year. The teams are cross-functional and try to accommodate people from all shifts, which sometimes means planning meetings at odd times. Navistar aims to have representation from HR, medical, safety, IT, union, nonunion, management and others who represent the different divisions of the organization.

"As wellness professionals, our job is to give them support and give them tools," Weddle says. One tool is a wellness audit, a thorough review that is conducted each year. That gives each team a framework in which to plan their health and wellness efforts. The committee uses this as a blueprint. Other tools are monthly e-mail communications, conference calls where members can share best practices, and planning material that is available within a password-protected Web site that only team members can access.

It's always valuable to share best practices instead of recreating the wheel. If a team wants to do a project such as a walking challenge, Weddle recommends that team members check with other groups to see if they have done anything similar and then take the best ideas from them.

Jennifer Flynn, a health management strategy consultant with Mayo Clinic Health Solutions, says companies ought to seek out "champions who have the personal motivation to take the extra step, who are energetic." She estimates that one to five percent of an organization's population should be wellness champions and believes that the organization should promote this network of champions so that there's a real sense of honor in being part of the group.

Company managers should make sure these champions have real input and define what their roles and responsibilities are. "Do you want [him/her] to do program planning? Promote activities among co-workers? Be the leader of a walking group? What are the responsibilities that person is signing on to? Let them know how much of a time commitment, so they clearly understand their role," she says.

Ed Buffett agrees that it's important to be candid with employees about what is involved in committee work. "This is a critical group. It's a mistake to get people on the committee without giving them an understanding of the commitment. Be up front with people," says Buffet. From his experience, he finds that most wellness teams tend to be busiest during the fall because it's often enrollment time, and in the spring when workers start being interested in outdoor activities.

It's also critical for committee members to work closely with your organization's wellness professionals, who can help determine what initiatives to roll out and develop good communications strategies. It's their expertise that can guide the committee and aid members in deciding the kinds of things that must be considered when making decisions about wellness initiatives.

If the company doesn't have an internal wellness professional, Buffett recommends finding a good wellness vendor to act as facilitator. "There has to be somebody knowledgeable in this area who can be a driver, a motivator, an enabler, a facilitator, a resource," he says.

Inevitably, turnover will thin the ranks of your wellness team, so it's always a good idea to be on the lookout for new prospects. Invite potential new members to meetings or to help out with events. And allow members who have been contributing less to step down gracefully.[3]

CHECK THE CLIMATE

There's no point in playing Russian roulette with your wellness dollars. Your committee needs good data to work with so it knows which initiatives have the best chance of succeeding.

TARGET THE SICK—OR THE WELL?

Once your team has conferred with management, surveyed employees, and perhaps conducted health assessments (see chapter 6), it's time to face the biggest question in wellness today: do you focus the majority of your time and money on the sickest employees or do you concentrate on keeping healthy people well?

Here's probably the most commonly cited statistic in health-care costs: 80 percent of an organization's health-related expenses can be attributed to 20 percent of the employees. Does that mean you should give your greatest attention to that 20 percent? Or should you pick the low-hanging fruit by keeping the 80 percent healthy? After all, these are the employees who are most productive.

The lion's share of the effort used to be directed at the sickest, "but that is the kind of thinking that got us into this mess in the first place," claims Dr. Dee W. Edington, director of the University of Michigan Health Management Research Center. "So we don't need more doctors, more nurses, more hospitals—we need fundamental change. And part of that is focusing on keeping the low-risk at low-risk."[4]

If your team concentrates primarily on the high-risk population, nothing ever changes. "By the time someone gets sick, they are swallowed up by the health-care system—and when they get the treatments, therapies, and medications they need, they disappear. Then, the next person gets sick and the process starts all over again. The only solution is to get to people before they become high-risk,"[5] he says.

So the trend now is to give more attention to keeping low-risk employees at low-risk status. These preventive efforts can provide high value by improving lives at a relatively low cost when compared with the expense of medical treatment.

Prevention is the goal of primary care, says Dr. Raymond J. Fabius, strategic advisor to the president of Walgreen's Health and Wellness division. A vaccine program is an example of primary care, one with an extraordinary return on investment.

Secondary care means catching a condition in the early stages to mitigate the impact and reduce morbidity. For example, mammograms and colonoscopies do not prevent cancer but can detect it at a more effectively treatable stage.

Tertiary care means treating someone who has a disease or condition. "Those of us who were focused on tertiary care now are focusing on secondary and primary care, on keep healthy people healthy," Dr. Fabius says. More and more, that's being seen as the best way to improve the health of Americans and reduce the financial and social burdens imposed by preventable diseases.

"Take the temperature of the organization," recommends Brandi Jessemy Whitney, a health promotion coordinator for the DeKalb County (Georgia) Board of Health. By that she means look at the climate, the culture. Is it formal or informal? It is a traditional business corporate culture of work, work, work? Has it been receptive to wellness initiatives in the past? Have there been little challenges, any little seeds that have worked? If there haven't been any at all, that tells you something as well.

Observe, have conversations, do interviews and focus groups with employees, Whitney advises. Get leadership buy-in, then set programmatic, measurable goals that align with corporate goals such as improving productivity and morale and being an employer of choice.

You may want to test the waters with a small pilot initiative, such as a corporate walk or run, to tell you if your organization is ready for bigger change, she says. Be sure to keep management informed of your efforts. Especially if it's a large organization, they may not be aware of small, but significant, programs.

Look at the health conditions in the community where your employees work and find out if your worksite is a microcosm of that community. Also look at the health threats that are most in the news because they may raise issues with your employees and be prominent on their radar screen. Some companies request or require that their employees take annual health assessments (see chapter 6) to get aggregate information about the greatest health risks their population faces.

Simply surveying employees is another great way to find out what they need—and want—from your wellness program. It's also true that employees who have input are more likely to participate. Just be sure to follow up on your surveys with concrete action.

Ask questions that really home in on employee availability and interest. You can carefully identify risk factors, but if nobody is interested in attending a program, then you're just throwing good money away. Work to develop a range that will both address primary health risks and appeal to the interests of the people.

When trying to determine the needs and wants of employees, make sure your efforts reflect the culture of your workplace. Surveys work well with in some cultures, but not all. "The most important thing you do is to get information from employees. That helps to get buy-in from them because they can see you are working on initiatives that meet their needs," says Joan Parks-Hubley.

Online survey tools are readily available to help you determine your employees' wellness concerns, but, again, know your climate. Are your employees comfortable with technology? Would they be more at ease with paper and pencil?

Whether paper or online, a survey shouldn't seem onerous. Don't make it too long; 20 questions is probably about right. Ask yourself: What is the intent of the survey? What questions do we *need* to ask to get those answers? You don't want people to think you are prying, and you don't want more data than you need. If you don't use it, why did you collect it?

"People ask us: How long is it going to take to do this? We try to keep it short," Parks-Hubley says. "If you hand people a packet, they start to shut down." Give people an idea at the start how long the survey is or they may abandon it when they're almost done, not realizing that they are near the end.

STAY ON TRACK

Once your wellness program is up and running, the committee's job is to keep it going in the right direction. The committee should periodically evaluate and fine tune programs as the make up and needs of the workforce changes.

The Energy Corporation of America in Charleston, West Virginia, polls employees to find out what's working—and what's *not* working. With each program, ECA conducts some type of satisfaction survey. "We ask: What changes could we make? How could it be modified?" says Wellness Director Kelly Sadd. "What would make it more appealing? If someone didn't participate, what might encourage them to participate in the next one? What are the overriding issues and how can I develop programs that address those issues?" ECA, with about 285 employees, is a 2008 winner of the C. Everett Koop National Health Award.

Wellness is just one of the issues addressed by the Staff Advisory Committee (SAC) of Porter Keadle Moore, LLP, an Atlanta-based public accounting firm. SAC representatives from all departments meet each month and voice concerns about everything from insurance issues to "What are we going to do for a holiday party?" "What about wearing jeans on Friday?" "What charity will we support?" But it's wellness—mental as well as physical—that is "a hot button right now," says Debbie Sessions, partner and chief operating officer. "We're trying to develop a program around a wellness challenge for the busy [tax] season from January to April. We want to develop a program that will be a wellness challenge, something personal like losing weight or developing a hobby" to relieve stress, she says. Everyone who meets the challenge will be eligible for a drawing to win a trip.

This concern for mental and well as physical health is what made Porter Keadle Moore a 2008 winner of the American Psychological Association's Psychologically Healthy Workplace Award. Porter Keadle Moore surveys employees every other year to see if improvements have been made in various categories. When one survey indicated that employees did not believe they were receiving enough timely feedback, the company initiated a feedback challenge in which it trained everyone on how to give and receive feedback and then set up a competition to encourage feedback with prizes awarded for those who excelled in the feedback initiative.

At Healthwise, another of the APA's Psychologically Healthy Workplace Award winners, the wellness team's main challenge is to keep the momentum going. The Boise, Idaho–based publisher of consumer health information already makes it easy for employees to exercise. The company has a fitness room, locker rooms with showers, company bikes, and on-site exercise and yoga classes and is near hiking and biking trails. Healthwise also makes it easy to relax. It has two quiet rooms for naps, nursing, and so forth; a sun deck; outdoor dining; a hammock; and on-site chair massages.

The company encourages work/life balance with flextime and telecommuting. It sponsors family oriented events such as picnics and a Halloween party where children receive noncandy treats. Employees can even bring their dogs to work.

The full team of volunteers meets every other month and assigns committees to work on specific projects. After each project there's a debriefing. "We want to make sure people have a sense of ownership, not just entitlement. They need to assume responsibility for wellness," says Molly Mettler, Healthwise senior vice president of mission and executive council liaison to the wellness committee.

SELL IT

Committee members are responsible for communicating the wellness message effectively and even for reassuring their coworkers, because sometimes employees get nervous about wellness programs. Maybe a person is a smoker or is overweight and wonders, "Is that going to cause me to lose my job down the line? Am I going to be penalized?" Committee members are exactly the right ones to reassure concerned coworkers, because the committee person who works on the line is likely to have the best understanding of how to communicate to people with similar roles within the organization.

Every committee member is also a missionary. In addition to sitting at the table and making decisions, committee members need to create some excitement, some enthusiasm in their respective groups about what is about to unfold. They need to get people excited, to be ambassadors to the program. They can accomplish their mission through word of mouth and through the company intranet.

And committee members are great conduits for feedback from the rest of the workforce. For example, if you are revamping the food in the cafeteria so that it offers healthy meals, committee members should be the ones explaining why it's being done and giving other employees an opportunity to offer their suggestions.

It's a two-way communication. Committee members are explaining the rationale for programs and also listening to the comments, both positive and negative. They are bringing messages back to the table about what people viewed as success and areas that need to be improved on. This back-and-forth gives people the opportunity to share their wellness stories and to talk about the changes they have been able to accomplish, so the good news gets out there on voluntary basis. You will find that people are happy to share.

TRAIN YOUR CREW

You'll want to offer training to get your team members started. There may be plenty of wellness information online, but don't take it for granted that everybody knows how to access those tools and use them. So make sure members have tools they can use and tutorials to help them learn new ones. And make sure committee members understand the full range of benefits available to everybody. As an example, Fiona Gathright of Wellness Corporate Solutions, notes that "people tend to overlook that insurance companies provide a lot of wellness benefits" to plan participants.

Training makes the committee members feel more empowered and directed, says Jennifer Flynn. Give them tool kits with a binder of information that spells out the goals of the program and the team members' responsibilities.

Don't forget rewards, to keep committee members active. Some companies give special incentives to their team members, who may not be eligible for the prizes other employees receive for participating in wellness events. "Maybe a paper certificate or a tee shirt they can wear at events. Or a letter from the CEO or other leadership that thanks them" for their work, suggests Flynn. "A nameplate. Simple things. What we hear works is to recognize these folks as leaders and facilitators of these programs."

Navistar works hard to keep its hardworking teams motivated, Dawn Weddle says, by offering them incentives to hit specific targets such as increasing participation in certain programs. Competitions where a team can win a free lunch or car washes or massages also help keep them involved.

The company has an annual meeting for the wellness volunteers at its Chicago-area headquarters where top executives speak about the importance of wellness. They share the business case for health promotion as well as their vision for a healthier Navistar. Weddle describes the annual meeting as fun filled and motivating, a celebration to fill the teams with the new energy they need to take back to their sites. You need to take care of your teams so they don't get burned out.

Most wellness professionals will tell you, as trite as it might seem, that this needs to be fun. Yes, it's serious business and it's work, but it needs to be fun in order to continue to engage committee members.

THE BOTTOM LINE

A well-organized, representative team is a valuable weapon in your fight for wellness. Make sure team members know what they're getting into and—through surveys—make sure they know what employees want and need. Set your team to work determining an overall strategy with clear objectives. Use your team members to sell the program their peers. Have the team periodically evaluate your wellness program and, if necessary, make adjustments. And don't forget to give your committee members a little TLC for all their hard work.

Now, with senior management onboard and a wellness team in place, it's time to get your feet wet. Chapter 4 shows you how.

Profile: USAA Ensures Success with Wellness Council (http:www.usaa.com)

USAA relies on its Wellness Council to make sure that its multidiscipline, integrated health and productivity management program runs smoothly. The Council must be doing something right. USAA, an insurance financial services provider to members of the U.S. military and their families, is a winner of the prestigious C. Everett Koop National Health Award. And the company estimates that its wellness efforts increased productivity by 187,200 hours over a one-year measurement period.

USAA's comprehensive program, "Take Care of Your Health," takes on a lot. Its components includes health assessments, lifestyle coaching, end-smoking efforts, and health improvement campaigns. To promote physical activity, the company provides access to fitness centers. It sponsors wellness breaks twice a week and offers nutritious food choices in cafeterias and vending machines. Incentives to employees who practice healthy lifestyles include reduced pricing on healthy foods and snacks, and a tiered rebate based on the number of times an employee works out in the fitness center each year.

The company is headquartered in San Antonio, Texas, and has five major offices around the country. In all there are 22,000 USAA employees around the world.

"Five years ago we didn't have a cohesive effort," says Dr. Peter Wald, USAA vice president and enterprise medical director. "For us to do our 'Take Care of Your Health' program, which is pretty complex, we need a lot of people to help us. . . . We use wellness as our primary prevention program. It involves everything we do to keep employees and their families healthy," says Wald.

So Wald and his staff, "collected everyone we needed" throughout the company into a diverse Wellness Council. Among those collected to work with the full-time wellness staff, according to Wald, are "the people who run the on-site fitness program. Food services, which reports to corporate services, is an important part of the effort. The safety department is another important part," especially in the area of preventing occupational disease and injuries.

The Council includes representatives from the corporate communications and corporate real estate office because sometimes "we need permission to change facilities or add facilities." It has "good engagement from the C-suite," Wald reports, with the executive vice president of people services acting at its "executive sponsor."

When ramping up many of the initiatives in 2005, the Wellness Council met once or twice a month, but "now we have meetings with the executive sponsor four times a year and meet as a Council about four times a year in between," Wald says.

In addition, the staff meets with individual components of the Council, such as food services or safety, to discuss particular issues. The Wellness Council "is an enterprise effort," Wald says, which operates "is like a project work team, without a sunset date."

The company now has more than 20 wellness initiatives and activities and has achieved high participation rates with about 85 percent of employees engaged in some way. About 60 percent of USAA's employee take on-site or on-line health assessments.

"Take Care of Your Health," includes a number of features:

- USAA cafeterias offer healthy take-home meals.
- The company stores stock items that encourage healthy behavior—cookbooks with nutritious recipes, pedometers, and exercise DVDs.
- Company recreational opportunities such as soccer and softball teams, employee bicycling and running clubs, and tennis leagues encourage employees to be more physically active.[6]

Employees who are eligible for the $350 wellness incentive (plus an extra $50 if they take part in a health assessment) can use the money to pay for weight management and fitness center activities or can use it to pay for dependents to enroll in the smoking cessation program.

"Take Care of Your Health" is seeing positive results beyond the productivity boost. Employees who participate in wellness programs in smoking cessation, physical activity, and weight reduction have experienced statistically significant decreases in their individual risk profile and their consumption of health-care dollars. USAA has held its overall employee cost increase to 5 percent total for four years.

USAA's wellness program is driven by data. Some companies rely mainly on employee surveys and feedback to monitor the effectiveness of their efforts, but USAA uses its own customized collection system that can capture workforce data such as demographics, participation rates, health and disability plan costs, and the success of program recommendations.

"We practice a metric-driven benefit design. We look at participation, financial returns and risk-factor reduction." Wald says. After looking at the data, "we decide whether a program is working or not working," he says, and new initiatives are introduced "where we see a need. The interventions match the target."

USAA's knows its target audience well. Its average worker is 38 years old and female, so "to be doing a full blown prostate cancer screening, for us, doesn't make any sense," he says. Instead, USAA offers more initiatives on breast cancer awareness and maternal and pregnancy health. There are between 800 and 1,200 babies born to USAA employees each year, Wald says, "so we talk about nutrition, about high-risk pregnancy. We have a very broad nursing mothers program for when women come back to work."

Wald credits the company's sophisticated data warehouse with enabling USAA to "watch what's happening very closely so that we can make adjustments that ultimately will improve the health of our employees and their families."

Chapter Four

Take the Plunge

You don't have to have an Olympic-size swimming pool to plunge into wellness. You can start with little money and no special facilities. Get senior management on board, form your wellness committee, survey your employees, and you're ready to get your feet wet.

Start with educating people about how to lead healthier lives. The phrase often used by health experts—*modifiable lifestyle behaviors*—may not have a dramatic ring, but it holds the key to healthier workers and lower costs. Begin simply by educating your workers about how to lead healthier lives and, specifically, how they can change behavior that is very likely to *damage* their health. Unhealthy lifestyle practices account for 90 percent of adult-onset diabetes cases, 80 percent of coronary heart disease cases, and 70 percent of stroke and colon cancer cases.[1]

You can help employees learn to change unhealthy behaviors by organizing seminars, brown-bag lunches, lunch-and-learns, or whatever you want to call them. Good topics to cover include nutrition and diet, fitness and exercise, stress reduction, and relaxation. For best results, however, you should gear the topics to your workforce. For example, if your employees are predominately female, you may want to have sessions covering diseases that are prevalent among woman, such as breast cancer. If the workforce is predominately male, employees could benefit from a session discussing prostate cancer. With a blue-collar workforce, you'll want to stress information on safety and injury prevention.

So before you start, survey your employees to find out what topics most interest them, then tailor your sessions to meet those needs. Provide them with resources about where they can find more information on their own about fitness, nutrition, and stress management.

Working through your wellness committee, have employees themselves create, organize, and promote the educational sessions to give them the sense of ownership and accountability. Never forget that employees are more likely to attend a voluntary event that's been arranged by their peers than by their managers.

The timing of the workshops will be different for each organization. The important point here is to make sure the meetings are accessible to all staff. This means that for organizations that work around the clock, you may want to consider breakfast, lunch, and evening sessions.

For example, since many of the 12,000 employees at Purolator Courier are truck drivers, activities are offered before shifts begin, and educational programs are online. And IBM Canada, with multiple locations, allows employees to connect from their various worksites.

Once your sessions are scheduled, spread the word with bright visual posters, targeted e-mails, and face-to-face reminders. Provide employees with a list of resources related to the topic of the day. Use the carrot approach to get people to attend by tossing in a healthy snack. Carrots, in fact, might be ideal, along with other veggies and/or fruit. This is not the occasion to spring for doughnuts.

Later, ask people why they chose to participate in a particular seminar or lunch-and-learn and find out what related topics might interest them. Don't forget to talk with employees who don't take part in activities, to learn what might draw them in. Use the information you gather to tweak programs. Continuous improvement works for wellness too.

IBM Canada held about 15 wellness education programs in 2005, "everything from eating to living well to protecting yourself from the sun to how to balance your life and handling workplace stress," says Wendy M. Howe, manager of benefits and well-being services.

Purolator takes advantage of local health department offerings on things such as heart disease and stroke. The company's lunch-and-learns also reflect seasonal concerns. During the flu season, it has held sessions on the importance of hand washing, and before the holidays, it has offered programs on nutrition and sensible eating.

Dr. Larry Catlett, medical director of Occupational Medical Consulting in Leeds, Maine, says his experience has taught him that most people already know they should stop eating fatty food and should exercise more. The real challenge is motivating them to take action.

The worst thing you can do is play expert, Catlett says. Anything that sounds like lecturing just pushes people to defend their behavior and resist change. "The traditional model is confrontational and people are in denial. You're making them mad," he says.

Catlett also cautions against trying to persuade employees to look after their own health when the company does not provide a supportive environment. If you give a lunch-and-learn on nutrition and your company cafeteria and vending machines are stocked with junk food, you're just giving a double message, Catlett warns. People are looking for things to fail, because that gives them an excuse not to participate.

DOWNSIZE YOUR WORKFORCE

In the United States, the most common health problem is weight. About 34 percent of American adults, or more than 72 million people, are obese.[2] Obesity—defined by the National Institutes of Health as a body mass index of 30 or above—currently costs U.S. companies an estimated $13 billion per year.[3]

Does that mean it's time to shrink your workforce, so to speak? ESI, a manufacturer of business telephone systems in Plano, Texas, thinks so. ESI launched "The Downsize Program" several years ago, working in conjunction with the Center for Lifestyle Enhancement at Medical Center of Plano.

It began as a simple, short-term project. Every week employees received packets of information about exercise and nutrition. The wellness team gave employees plenty of ideas and resources, but individuals could choose whatever type of weight-management program they wanted.

"We outlawed snacks at the office. We started with a 10-week moratorium, asking that there be no bowls of candy on desks," says Becki Veal, ESI director of human resources. After the moratorium ended, the candy bowls never came back.

The company switched from setting out bagels and sugary pastries at meetings to serving fresh fruit. "The first time I thought they were going to throw it at me," Veal says, but "people are now more health conscious. They watch out for each other," and offer encouragement.

The pounds fell off, Veal reports. Doug Boyd, ESI's president and COO, lost about 20 pounds. "It's been really good for everybody. It has impacted our insurance. We didn't do it just for that, but that's a great benefit," she says.

As the waistlines shrank, the original 10-week program was extended, running from January almost to July. Of the people who lost weight in that first year, none have gained it back, Veal says, because they also changed their lifestyles. Employees generally lost weight slowly, only one or two pounds a week, so it stayed off. ESI resumed its program the following January, just in time to help with New Year's resolutions.

Some companies rely on fellowship and competition to lighten up the workforce by sponsoring weight loss contests much like the reality television shows *The Biggest Loser* and *Celebrity Fit Club*. If you choose a competition, help participants set reasonable goals and focus on long-term results, not just on quick weight loss.

People often appreciate some type of weigh-in because the accountability factor keeps them from backsliding, but to protect privacy, consider tracking only the weight loss of the entire group, or of rival teams, but not of individuals.

To motivate participants in the weight-management program at the Center for Lifestyle Enhancements, each participant contributes a $50 check, and every week during the program that the person loses weight, he/she gets $5 back. "If they don't lose, they forfeit $5" per week, says Mary Jo Stellano, corporate contract coordinator for the Center for Lifestyle Enhancement. The money collected is then either split among the top three biggest losers by percentage of weight lost or donated to a local charity.

The program has been set up that way because it is easy to implement and employees don't have to attend weekly meetings, Stellano says. There are plenty of other weight-loss program options to offer employees, like Weight Watchers at Work, she notes, that offer more personalized attention and the opportunity for group discussion and interaction. Offering a couple of options simultaneously can address employees' different learning styles and desired time and financial commitment.

"To avoid embarrassment, we don't post information about individual weight loss using real names. We post weight loss by an 'alias.' It's a fun way to see how everyone from Madonna to Brad Pitt are doing and keeps everyone working a little harder," Stellano says.

Before deciding what approach to take to weight management— just as with any other wellness program—conduct a needs assessment and ask employees what would work best for them . . . and when. "If you think you're the know it all, you'll quickly find out you could be highly mistaken. You can put all this energy into a program and find that no one gets involved," Stellano says.

The Center makes sure that retired workers and family members can also participate in the programs. The Center has someone act as liaison with retirees, and using newsletters and a Web site link retirees are notified of screenings, behavior modification programs, and educational opportunities. She finds it's relatively easy to stay in contact with people.

People often know they need to take steps to control their weight but don't know how to get started, so Texas Instruments Inc. provides a combination of nutrition education, exercise, and behavioral modification. The Dallas-based company, two-time winner of the National Business Group on Health's Best Employers for Healthy Lifestyles, offers both on-site education and software that employees can put on their home computers.

The emphasis is on losing weight slowly, just a pound or two a week, says Linda Moon, manager of health promotion and wellness at Texas Instruments. And "we really try to tie in a lot of our other resources such as the Employee Assistance Program because stress can contribute to weight problems," she says.

The network of registered dietitians who provide individualized nutrition counseling is available not only to TI employees, but to retirees and dependents as well. The weight-management program is designed to engage the entire family because an individual employee doesn't have as much success if people at home aren't supportive, Moon says.

People are dying of poor lifestyle choices, not infectious diseases. It all comes down to down to personal responsibility. The basic problem is: we eat too much and we're not active enough. We need subtle reminders. Sometimes it's the simplest things that motivate the best.

PUT VENDING MACHINES ON A DIET

It doesn't do much good to bring in dietitians and nutritionists if you keep the workplace larded with sweet, salty, and fatty food. So take steps to give employees more nutritious options and fewer temptations in vending machines and/or the company cafeteria.

In the cafeteria, you don't have to replace what one wellness expert likes to call the Mercy Burger—lord have mercy if you eat it—with lettuce leaves, but make sure at least some lower-fat options are available.

Have your vending machines stocked with animal crackers; nuts; and fresh, dried, and canned fruit. Take out some of the candy, cookies, pastries, regular chips, and pork rinds. Reduce the amount of regular soft drinks, sports drinks, and whole milk and replace them with water, juice, and low-fat milk.

When you decide to make the switch, replace just a few items at first. To ensure buy-in and ownership of the changes, survey employees about what they to might like to see added or deleted. Don't be afraid to subsidize the healthier choices by boosting the price of unhealthy items in the cafeteria and vending machines. Promote the healthy choices and advertise your success. Send out memos; put articles on your Web site or in newsletters.

When Texas Instruments decided to stock its vending machines with healthier items, vendors worried that those items wouldn't sell. So the company at first required suppliers to ensure that 30 percent of the items in vending machines were relatively nutritious. People were receptive enough to the change that TI increased it to 50 percent.

At Health Alliance Plan (HAP), a nonprofit health plan in southeastern Michigan, sometimes employees can smell nutritious meals as they're being prepared. In addition to bringing in nutritionists to speak and having a dietitian on hand for consultations, HAP has hosted a personal chef to demonstrate how to prepare recipes ranging from vegetable stroganoff to smoothies.

"People loved the cooking demo. The chef showed realistic meals that working people can do, not meals that take four hours to prepare," says Mary Carley, former health promotion coordinator. HAP promotes Five a Day for Better Health—an adaptation of the Produce for Better Health Foundation's program Five a Day the Color Way. The foundation encourages people to eat more deeply hued fruits and vegetables because they provide the wide range of vitamins, minerals, fiber, and phytochemicals that protect against the effects of aging and reduce the risk of cancer and heart disease. The goal is to eat at least five servings a day of foods such as apples, blackberries, blueberries, broccoli, cranberries, green peppers, oranges, spinach, and tomatoes.

HAP turned its Five a Day program into a contest in which employees tracked the amount of fruits and vegetables they ate. At the end of the six-week contest there was a drawing with prizes such as dinner for two at home with that popular personal chef.

WALK THIS WAY

Encouraging employees to eat more nutritious food is only part of the cure. With physical activity at an all-time low in the United States, most people aren't getting enough exercise to stay healthy. You can help employees get and stay in better physical shape by sponsoring simple exercise programs that encourage them to be just a little more active each day.

A study on the effects of exercise on overweight, middle-aged people found that a half-hour long, brisk walk six days a week was enough to reduce their waistlines and the risk of metabolic syndrome. Metabolic syndrome is not itself a disease but is a group of risk factors, such as abdominal obesity and insulin resistance, which puts a person in greater danger of coronary heart disease.

"It's encouraging news for sedentary, middle-aged adults who want to improve their health. It means they don't have to go out running four or five days a week; they can get significant health benefits by simply walking around the neighborhood after dinner every night," says study leader Johanna L. Johnson, a clinical researcher at Duke University Medical Center, Durham, North Carolina.[4]

One of the easiest ways to help your employees start on the road to a healthier, more active life is a step-counting program. In a step-counting program, people wear pedometers from morning until night, logging the number of steps they take each day and building on that number. Step counting can be done by any interested individual; it also makes a great activity for groups of employees.

Walking about 10,000 steps, about five miles a day, is the optimum figure for managing weight, according to Shape Up America, founded by former Surgeon General C. Everett Koop. The average white-collar employee moves an estimated 3,500 steps per day— slightly more than one mile.

Michigan's Health Alliance Plan (HAP) has sponsored a number of walking programs. The first year, "we had a challenge, and having pedometers as a way to measure steps helped. The competitiveness of the staff played into it and made it fun," Mary Carley says.

Before the kick off, the wellness team gave members of upper management tee shirts and whistles and made them coaches so they felt involved. "We asked them to wear the shirts on the two days we held the sign up," she says. Although employees were walking on their own time, upper management's participation gave employees the reassurance that they had their bosses' support for the event. Carley and all the members of the wellness committee joined in the walk. Each week employees got an update of their progress.

At the end of the first challenge, workers at one company site had walked 7,161 miles, which is the distance from Detroit to Shanghai, China. Workers at a second site walked 16,207 miles, which is comparable to walking from Southfield to Nairobi, Kenya, to Sydney, Australia.

The only real drawback was that, with more than 500 people turning in logs during the challenges, tracking everyone's progress was cumbersome. Carley recommends involving the IT department in tracking results, if possible.

People loved the camaraderie of the competition and the fitness-related results, telling Carley "I lost 10 pounds" and "I'm off my hypertension medicine." Informally, the journey continues. HAP keeps signs in the lobbies that an employee can put up when he or she has the urge to lead a walk.

Texas Instruments started its on-site walking program in 2005, complete with a walking path. The program is designed so people can participate on their own or in groups and so family members can join in as well.

The company supplies pedometers and log books—and motivation through weekly e-mail messages and prize drawings. There's a Web site so participants can log in and they and the company can track information. "We can get aggregate information and understand the impact" on employee health, Linda Moon says.

Purolator Courier, which is based in Mississauga, Ontario, and has about 125 facilities across Canada, promotes walking through a joint program with Running Room, a retailer that sells shoes and equipment. Running Room has running clubs and walking clubs at its outlets, and Purolator provides a link to the Running Room Web site on their Healthy Workplace Web page, says Doug Kube, former director of environmental health, safety and security. Running Room offers a guide on how to warm up, and Purolator Courier employees access its intranet site to measure and track performance. Employees also have access to an online coach.

Participants in the Pikes Peak Challenge at Health and Hospital Corporation of Marion County, Indiana, are allowed to track many types of movement, which are then converted into steps. Bowling, for example, counts as 87 steps per minute, while moderate swimming counts as 175 steps. Participants can rack up steps working as well as playing. Washing the car counts for 85 steps per minute, while shoveling snow equals 175 steps per minute.

The goal for participants is to virtually reach the summit of Pikes Peak, a journey of 2,230,000 steps from Indianapolis. The organization's goal, according to Human Resource Manager Andy Scott, was to develop a movement and activities program that included as many employees as possible on a budget of less than $500 for 800 employees.

STEPPING UP AND OTHER IDEAS

A really inexpensive approach is to turn company stairways into exercise opportunities. Lifting your body against gravity to climb stairs is one of the best exercises around for heart, muscles, and bones. Yale University obesity expert Kelly Brownell estimates that walking up and down two flights of stairs just once a day for a year will keep off six pounds.

Post information in the stairwells about other wellness programs. You might even try hiding prizes in stairways to encourage employees to use them. A word of caution though—most stairways are part of the building's emergency/fire evacuation system and therefore subject to fire and life safety code restrictions. To avoid problems later, before making any changes to existing stairways, consult with your local, county, or state fire marshal.

A few organizations, such as the American Psychological Association, have created labyrinths—intricate patterned walkways where employees can meditate as they stroll.

Biking is a key component of Anheuser-Busch Brewers' Ability for Life wellness program. The overall program stresses personal responsibility—good nutrition, exercise and conditioning, regular health exams, and the use of car seat belts and bicycle helmets. Anheuser-Busch employees and friends ride together as Team Michelob ULTRA to raise funds for Multiple Sclerosis Society and Special Olympics.

How you pitch the programs to employees matters. At Purolator Courier, exercise classes are promoted to appeal to the mainly male workforce. "We introduced a 'sweatless' workout. You just need a meeting room to do yoga, Pilates and Tai Chi. But it's how you market it. If we said we were offering yoga, it probably wouldn't fly, so we tell them it's stretching, that it prepares them for their work activities or preferred sport, like hockey or soccer," says Doug Kube.

And consider the age of your workforce. "People in their 50s are saying 'I need to do something,' but they aren't going to be running and playing hockey. They can do a sweatless workout," Kube says.

Other employers offer classes ranging from simple stretching to energetic cardio boxing to fit all kinds of interests and needs. Yoga is especially in vogue—Nike, HBO, Forbes, and Apple all offer on-site yoga classes for their employees, according to *Yoga Journal.* Subsidized or free gym or swim club memberships are always popular, as are company sponsored softball or volleyball teams.

Employees might want to try corporate ballroom dancing or learn to *conductorise* (http://www.conductorise.com), which bills itself as a way to "relieve stress, build aerobic stamina, and shed unwanted pounds, while imagining yourself leading a symphony orchestra."

Chesapeake's Energy Corp. employees can earn their scuba-diving certification at classes in the company's on-site Olympic-size pool. The Oklahoma City company hires the instructor and pays the bill.[5]

Why not take programs directly to the people? That's what William Baun, manager of the human resources and wellness at the University of Texas Hospital in Houston, does with his wellness-on-wheels cart filled with useful materials.

Baun goes out to office corridors and puts up a sign, "Wellness Coach on Duty" and provides materials and advice because he says he can reach more people this way than by waiting for them to come to his office. He also holds "ASAP" meetings in the hallways under the slogan, "If you have five to 10 minutes, we will advance your knowledge."[6]

Workers don't even need to walk down the hall to get more exercise. There are videos and tips for exercising at your desk, doing yoga at your desk, even dancing at your desk.

The Alberta Centre for Active Living, a government-funded organization based at the University of Alberta, scored itself a minor Internet hit with a series of videos including *Yoga @ Your Desk* and *Stretching @ Your Desk.* An office workout video produced by Sparkpeople.com offers a 15-minute routine that uses an office wall to do squats and turns a chair into a strength-training apparatus.

DanceAtYourDesk.com is a project by Elastic Illusion, a group of California break-dancers, that teaches workers how to do basic breakdance moves at their desks.[7]

Perhaps the trendiest choice is the walkstation, a piece of exercise equipment that allows employees to work at their computers while slowly walking on a treadmill. Office furniture maker Steelcase produced the walkstation based on research by James Levine at the Mayo Clinic. The walkstation provides benefits through a process called "'non-exercise activity thermogenesis' (NEAT), or incremental movements without strenuous exercise."[8]

THE BIG TENT

Bring all your wellness initiatives together under one tent and pump up employee enthusiasm by organizing a health fair. Health Alliance Plan (HAP) has been holding an annual health fair for several years, with activities including blood pressure screenings and presentations by the company's Employee Assistance Program, Weight Watchers, and the Work-Family Balance Center. Fitness Works, one of HAP's partner organizations, offers discounts to employees who attend the fair. Keep on the lookout for new activities to add to the health fairs. "You've got to spice it up a little. If you don't, they won't come every year," Carley says.

IBM Canada holds health fairs at more than a dozen company locations. The last time, "to encourage people we had a drawing for pedometers with IBM logos. People sent us thank-you notes," Howe says. "Pedometers are very linked to what we were trying to encourage"—employee participation in healthy activities.

Deffenbaugh Industries held a health fair in a landfill. That's because that's where the Shawnee Mission, Kansas–based waste management company has its headquarters. In other ways, the Deffenbaugh health fair resembled many others. Health-care professionals were on-site to administer screenings and distribute materials about how to reduce health risks. "There were people who didn't know they had diabetes, and they found out that day. One employee had a cholesterol count over 300 and now he's being treated," says Karrie Andes, HR director.[9]

In a twist on the health fair concept, Duke University holds a farmer's market once a week between 11 and 2, giving employees the opportunity to buy fresh local products. Employees who can't attend the farmers market can pick up boxes of produce through the university's "Mobile Market." The farmer's market "started as a way to incent people to eat fruits and vegetables," says Julie Joyner manager of the "Live for Life" program, which began in 1988. It's now seen as chance to give everyone a stress break, with employee-performed music during the event.

The university has "a huge focus on keeping healthy people healthy," says Joyner. That can be tricky with 26,000 benefits-eligible employees who work multiple shifts, so she's always looking for new ideas. The university has added "dinner on demand"—prepackaged healthy meals prepared by local chefs. Families are not eating together as much as they used to Joyner says, so the question is: "how can we make it easy to provide healthy quick meals?"

When looking for good vendors to provide wellness services at health fairs, you might start with local hospitals. "They have the widest range of health-care professionals. I'm not saying that independent vendors are not excellent, but a lot of employees are already being sent to the local hospitals" and are familiar with them, says Mary Jo Stellano. (See chapter 9 for more on low-cost resources.) She suggests that smaller companies that don't have a lot of resources check around their communities for free, local programs.

What's critical when working with vendors is to feel confident that a particular aspect of wellness is their specialty and to engage vendors who understand your culture. Communication must be very clear, so they know what you're looking for and what your expectations are. Follow up is important too. Introduce the vendors to one another so they can be familiar with each other's programs. They can be complementary to each other, and the multiple programs build on one another.

Send the message that there's a variety of ways to stay healthy, and employees start listening.

SPREAD THE WORD

Good communication is the key to success in the workplace and that certainly holds true for your wellness program. You can combine low-tech posters and newsletters with intranet and e-mail invitations to get your message across to employees.

Then, use their own words as testimonials. People are very happy, if they've had success, to tell their stories. Communicate those success stories through posters on display throughout your facilities, through quarterly newsletters to every employee at home, and through e-mail and Web sites.

More and more, it's technology that gets the wellness message out. The Web is a great place to direct employees to for more information about how to live healthier lives. WebMD (http://www. webmd.com), MyEphit (http://www.myephit.com), my Optum-Health (http://www.myoptumhealth.com), and HealthFitness (http://www.hfit.com) are among the most popular Web programs, and your company can customize the site without a lot of extra expense. Brand your site with your logo to give it a different look and feel.

Wellness information needs to be prominent on the Web site and shouldn't require too many clicks down to get to it. Once employees make their way to the site, they should find a number of interesting features, including perhaps key information about their benefit plans. And, with secure Web site mailboxes, you can use the site to provide individual confidential messages to employees about their health.

There's a move toward using Web portals to give reminders, says John Harris, principal of Harris HealthTrends, a wellness service company. "You can set it before lunchtime to remind you that you've committed yourself to staying away from fat or whatever," he says. "It can help keep in the forefront of your mind."

But just making information available doesn't do anything to hold people accountable for their behavior. Human interaction is the important component and you have to make sure that you use technology to enhance that.

For example, technology can bring people who are struggling with behavior issues together into one virtual community. A smoker with cravings at two o'clock in the morning can chat online with and get support from others. They can help each other 24/7.

Or, technology can help prompt people who want to lose weight. An individual can go to the Web site and read about losing weight and set a goal to lose 20 pounds. If the person doesn't come back to the Web site, there's a prompt to call a telephone coach.

Improvements in technology make it easier to assign telephone coaches to people whose behavior put them at risk. While personal one-on-one coaching is expensive, there are advantages to the telephone approach. There's the perceived anonymity, and people can get coaching in their pajamas.

QUICK BITES, SMALL STEPS

- Partner with local hospitals and nonprofit groups to get the message out about how to change unhealthy behaviors.
- Survey employees about their health concerns—and follow through with programs that address those concerns.
- Make health information available on your Web site.
- Serve fruit, not doughnuts, at company meetings.
- Offer more healthy items in vending machines.
- Host a farmer's market to bring in fresh produce.
- Arrange cooking demonstrations of nutritious meals.
- Give employees pedometers to measure their daily activity.
- Sponsor a walking club.
- Encourage employees to use the stairs.
- Give out small prizes, such as tee shirts and water bottles, for participating in exercise programs.
- Promote charity runs and walks that your employees can take part in.
- Hold a health fair.

As offices become less centralized and more employees telecommute, you might even want to host your health fair online. Dynamic Wellness in Chicago constructed a 3D layout called "Wellness Town" with a Nutrition Café, fitness center, clinic, and communications center to house the various elements of wellness content including video, e-learning, and webinars.

THE BOTTOM LINE

Let your employees know that better health doesn't have to be complicated. Heed that advice yourself. Start your wellness effort with basic educational programs that provide workers with information about how to lead healthier lives and, specifically, how they can change behaviors that are most likely to damage their health.

Survey your employees to find out what topics most interest them, then tailor your brown bag sessions to meet those needs. Encourage employees to eat healthier foods not only by providing information about nutrition but by removing some of the temptations lurking in company vending machines and cafeterias.

Help them get and stay in better physical shape by sponsoring simple exercise programs that encourage them to be just a little more active each day. Walking is great exercise, and a step-counting program is one of the easiest ways to start people on the road to a more active life. Turn your building's stairways into an urban gym. Encourage running, swimming, and biking. Offer classes and discounted gym memberships. Sponsor company sports teams.

Inform, encourage, but don't preach. Use technology to prod people into taking action and use it to share employee success stories. And consider offering employees incentives that will help them stay on track. Chapter 5 discusses how to motivate employees effectively—and legally.

Profile: Walk This Way (http://www.odscompanies.com)

Medical and dental insurance provider ODS Companies hit the ground running—make that walking—when it launched its wellness initiative in 2003. ODS put together a solid, basic package that focuses on physical activity, weight management, and health information.

To encourage both active and sedentary members of its 800 employee workforce to participate, the company started a walking program. And, to keep that program interesting, ODS mapped a "virtual walk" from the company's Portland, Oregon, headquarters across the state and later across America.

But first ODS mapped out an overall wellness plan that was simple, clinically sound, and cost effective. Its "Personal Best" initiative was the result of surveying employees, convening focus groups, organizing a wellness committee, and getting buy-in from front-line workers and senior managers alike.

The prescription for an effective wellness program, according to Dr. Csaba Mera, vice president and medical director, is that "promotion of the program and some of the activities have to be on company time. Top management has to be the driver. It has to be simple and inclusive and there have to be some kind of incentives to get people to participate."

The program's big step off featured Robert Sweetgall, president and founder of Creative Walking Inc. During 1984 and 1985, Sweetgall literally walked 11,208 miles through all 50 U.S. states, averaging 31 miles a day.

That big launch got people engaged and excited, Mera says, adding that the event was held on company time to show that wellness "is important enough that we're willing to pay for it." A senior vice president also spoke, to reinforce upper management's support.

ODS subsidized kits with pedometers and log books to record each step on the journey to better health. The first virtual journey lasted a year; some walkers logged enough miles to reach Iowa City, Iowa, nearly 2,000 miles away. For each 100 miles walked, employees received prizes such as fanny packs and water bottles; larger prizes were awarded at the 400-mile mark.

The next year, ODS launched a second virtual trek, this time to Whistler, British Columbia, with plans to extend the journey to Anchorage, Alaska, where the company has offices.

In its third year, ODS decided it was time for a change of pace. In response to feedback from employees, the company decided to arrange discounts to either a regular gym or to a less rigorous circuit-style gym. "We couldn't just say we're going to do another virtual journey. We had to freshen it up," says Mera.

The company gave employees access to Health Activity Tracker, a software program that allows them to tally up the calories burned by various activities — even walking the dog or mowing the lawn — accumulate points, and earn rewards.

In step with the physical activity component, ODS focuses on nutrition and weight management. ODS chose an alliance with Weight Watchers "because it was the most sensible, the one that least promoted any products. It has a long track record and is reasonably priced," according to Mera. ODS subsidizes the cost of Weight Watchers meetings, he notes, but "we didn't want to make it completely free because people wouldn't value it." So far, 130 participants have lost more than 3,500 pounds.

To encourage better eating habits, ODS phased in healthier food choices in its vending machines and brought in a nutritionist to demonstrate light cooking techniques. "It's a soft way to draw people to something better," Mera says.

The latest addition is Dream Meals, a company that provides the location, healthy ingredients, and nutritious recipes for people to quickly buy and assemble a week's worth of meals for themselves and their families. Employees put together their own quick, nutritious meals, which helps them avoid the temptation of fatty fast food. Weekly deliveries of fresh fruit to its three Oregon worksites complete the nutrition aspect of the wellness program.

The third prong of ODS's wellness program is education. Mera believes it's important to help employees understand their own medical conditions rather than simply doing what doctors tell them to do. If the patient is understands and is involved, the outcome is likely to be better.

ODS offers Healthwise (http://www.healthwise.org), a nonprofit online service, because "it's in easy-to-understand language and it walks you through alternative treatments," Mera says. "For example, if you have back problems it explains about choices, alternative treatments as well as surgery."

Employees and family members log in with a password to get quick health tips, take quizzes, and find out about a variety of medical conditions. The company put a computer in the lunch room so employees can use it on breaks or during lunch and people are encouraged to use the program at home as well.

ODS reinforces its wellness message on the company intranet and gives employees access to eDocAmerica (http://www.edocamerica.com), which includes a nurse advice hotline. Plus, Mera says, "We have our own disease management nurses, so employees can receive customized one-on-one coaching."

The company holds brown bag lunches on topics such as stress management, and every 18 months hosts health fairs with health screenings at all three of its Oregon locations.

Technology makes it possible to capture data without invading an individual's privacy, says Mera, allowing ODS to measure the success of its wellness program, using baseline measurements taken before the program started. It's results that count. Not only have employees walked thousands of miles and lost more than a ton and a half, but the company is saving money on health-care costs. When ODS compared the per member/per month cost 18 months prior to the beginning of the wellness program with the cost 18 months following the program's implementation, it found employee health claims trended at 5.8 percent compared to the overall industry trend of 12.2. percent.

ODS also found that unplanned personal leave days were significantly lower for wellness participants than for those who did not enroll. And for those who participated in both the walking and the weight-management elements of the wellness program, the use of unplanned personal leave days actually decreased 21 percent.

Chapter Five

Carrots and Sticks

An effective incentive program that engages your employees isn't as simple as just handing out free water bottles, but, in part because of clarifications in the Health Insurance Portability and Accountability Act, it doesn't have to be hopelessly complicated either.

Employers are jumping on the incentives bandwagon. About half of the companies in a 2008 survey were using incentives to encourage workers to participate in health-improvement activities such as weight-management or stop-smoking programs. By 2009, that number was expected to increase to 74 percent.[1] Some type of cash reward was most frequently cited as the incentive for participating in healthy activities, according to the survey by the National Business Group on Health and Watson Wyatt.

Employees seem to appreciate the extra boost incentives can give them to overcome their health problems and develop healthy habits. In another survey, this one by Guardian Life Insurance Company, 68 percent said they believe incentives can help them to shore up the willpower to adopt healthier behaviors.[2]

That's human nature. Most people require an added incentive to move out of their comfort zone and change thoroughly ingrained behaviors. Incentive programs are what set the other wheels in motion. They should deliver a consistent message and be designed as to reinforce your broader program strategy.[3]

SIMPLE CARROTS

A well-thought-out wellness incentive plan gives all employees a chance to take part and focuses on participation rather than on outcomes. You can offer token rewards like tee shirts and coffee mugs, but more imaginative incentives add appeal to your program and motivate both active and sedentary employees to participate. And that ultimately can lead to a larger return in health and productivity.

It's best to start off with a simple program. Don't bite off more than you can chew. Make it convenient to participate, using simple designs and giving financial incentives "to get people off the dime," says Michael F. Carter, vice president and regional director of the Hay Group.

Companies tend to implement too much in the first year. Get buy-in first; get people comfortable with the process. Debug—find out what doesn't work. Then you can roll out a more comprehensive plan.

Keep your incentive program fresh and upbeat. "Have contests with prizes a couple times a year. Add a little fun," Carter advises. "Add some sex appeal. Get people's attention."

Your incentive program should be structured to entice both high-risk and healthy employees. For too long, incentives have been one size fits all. That approach "is what killed wellness in the '80s and we're afraid it will kill the movement again if we don't . . . wake people up to the fact that we've got to get a whole lot more creative with incentivizing participation," says Bill Sims, president of Bill Sims Company.

You need more and larger incentives for medium- and high-risk employees than you do for low-risk employees, says Sims, whose company offers employee motivation and recognition programs. Low-risk employees may be happy enough to receive tee shirts and water bottles for activities that would have attracted them anyway, but high-risk employees—the ones who really push up the cost of health care—need more valuable, more imaginative rewards.[4]

Giving employees some choice in the rewards they receive can increase the effectiveness of the incentive, increasing participation rates and ultimately the success of the program. For example, participants at one company who recorded their physical activity were given tickets for every four hours of cumulative exercise recorded. They used the tickets to enter to win a grand-prize choice of a 42-inch television or a $5,000 travel gift certificate, as well as monthly prizes such as gift certificates to sport stores.

Flexibility was a key factor in the prize selection process. "Gift certificates were chosen, as they allow participants to pick their own prize rather than be dangled with an unappealing carrot. A choice among the grand prize was given for the same reasoning," says Kathleen Jones, a business manager with Fraser & Hoyt Incentives in Halifax, Nova Scotia, which helped design the campaign.

In spite of unusually bad weather during the program, the participation rate was almost 80 percent, and the company recorded a 21 percent decline in sick days, compared with the same time period the previous year. Morale and wellness goals were more than achieved, and employees gained an increased respect and commitment to physical activity. There was a lingering feeling of competitive excitement long after the campaign ended, Jones reports.

The Great American Insurance Group has gone to great lengths to encourage people to improve their health through exercise, screenings, and weight management. To kick off its first wellness campaign, Great American's parent company, American Financial Group, offered employees who participated in a six-month health challenge a chance to win some big-ticket items. The company agreed to give away these high-value incentives if at least 70 percent of employees participated in health screenings, and if overall scores were higher than the previous year. Winners were chosen randomly from all who participated, with a grand prize of a new convertible and other prizes such as $10,000 and $5,000 shopping sprees.

Cutting health costs is especially important to self-insured businesses, notes Vice President Scott Beeken. "If a single at-risk employee can avoid a triple bypass procedure, we'll save as much as $75,000 and enable that person to remain a happy and healthy member of the Great American family for years to come."[5]

POINTS ARE POPULAR

Allowing employees to earn points toward prizes by taking part in certain activities has become a popular way to encourage healthy behavior, and a number of health insurance companies now offer variations on that theme to their customers.

CIGNA has a points-based program called IncentOne's Health Power that offers incentives tied to various benchmarks, including the completion of a health assessment and biometric screenings, and participation in prevention programs that focus on such things as heart disease, diabetes, and depression, as well as lifestyle management programs such as smoking cessation. Employees can access their personal incentive accounts through a CIGNA Web portal and view such information as the types of programs available to them, the points they have earned for participation in the different programs, and the number of points they have redeemed.

Kaiser Permanente has a program that rewards people who complete health assessments and courses on stress management, nutrition, and/or weight loss. The company orders gift-card prizes from Amazon.com, Macy's, and 1-800-Flowers for gift-card options.

Completing a health assessment, signing up for an online weight-loss coach, getting an annual physical exam, or logging steps on a pedometer are all ways to earn points at Humana Inc. in Denver. Employees can trade in points for such things as movie-theater tickets, golf clubs, and gift cards to Best Buy or REI.

While most points programs are aimed at large companies, Humana's program shows that it can work well for small companies, ones with fewer than 100 employees.[6]

Using a points-system incentive program can help you better motivate your employees because it gives them flexibility about what rewards they receive for their wellness efforts.

CASH IS KING

Cash, of course, offers plenty of flexibility. Among the various types of incentives offered, cash-based rewards are the most popular. An estimated 67.8 percent of wellness managers used cash-based incentives in 2006.[7]

"It's real simple. Cash gets people's attention and we want to get people's attention," says Randy MacDonald, senior vice president, human resources of IBM. IBM's "Healthy Living" program is well known within the wellness management world. Big Blue started its incentives program with small prizes such as pedometers. In 2003, the company began offering a premium discount for nonsmokers and for smokers who completed a smoking cessation program.

The program has become much more comprehensive. It now offers employee $150 cash rebates; each employee can chose two of three possible rebate options to receive up to $300 in cash per year:

- Employees earn a physical activity rebate for participating in a 12-week physical activity program in which they exercise 30 minutes three times a week or take part in a weight-management program.

- After three successful years, the smoke-free rebate was replaced by a preventive-care rebate option. Employees receive the preventive-care rebate by taking a health appraisal, getting recommended screenings, and completing a Web-based interactive intervention on key health topics.
- Concerned that a third of American children and youths are obese or at risk of becoming obese, IBM has added a children's health rebate for U.S. employees to encourage healthy living for families and children as well as employees. The children's health rebate rewards good nutrition and physical activity for the entire family, which the company sees as key to helping children develop healthy habits for a lifetime.

In other parts of the world where IBM has a large number of employees, it has similar programs to encourage healthy behaviors, designed with a local twist to reflect the health issues and culture of each area.

PREMIUM INCENTIVES

Although cash is still king, in recent years there has been a significant shift to using lower medical premiums as an incentive.

Safeway Inc. gives rebates to its nonunion administrative employees who practice what the company preaches. Its wellness program, Healthy Measures, gives employees reductions in their insurance premiums if they are, and stay, within certain limits on four common medical risk factors—smoking, obesity, blood pressure and cholesterol. Rebates for making the grade on all four risk factors total nearly $800 a year for an individual employee, plus a similar amount for the employee's spouse or partner. No requirements are imposed on children covered through an employee's insurance, and medical exceptions are made for those with conditions that prevent reaching the goals.

People who tested within the limits got lower health premiums at the outset of the year, while those who missed one or more of the four goals can get a retroactive rebate if they improve sufficiently by the end of the year.[8] Using lower medical premiums as an incentive is particularly effective because it provides a direct linkage with the message you're sending—that you want employees to be healthier. Whether tying premiums to a healthy lifestyle is a carrot or a stick approach depends on your point of view, Hay Group's

Michael Carter says. He sees it as a carrot—employees pay lower health premiums if they participate in the organization's health management program.

Others see it a stick used to prod employees into giving up costly habits, particularly smoking and poor eating patterns that contribute to obesity, diabetes and high cholesterol. There's no doubt those habits are costly:

- An employer pays about $1,000 more in direct and indirect costs for an employee who smokes than for an employee who doesn't smoke, according to the American Lung Association.

- Obesity is estimated to cost U.S. companies $13 billion per year, according to the National Business Group on Health.

In an effort to help lower such costs, employees at Bank of Geneva in Indiana receive a $500 discount on their $3,000 yearly health insurance deductible if they don't smoke and another $1,500 in annual credits if they keep their weight, blood pressure, and cholesterol in check.

Andrew Briggs, the bank's president, sees this as a powerful motivating factor for employees to take care of themselves. "We're seeing people that want to get their deductibles down. They've got a goal and [they're] working toward it," Briggs says. "If you project it out at the rate of increase we were going in the last two years we've seen about a $400,000 savings."[9]

CAN YOU USE A STICK AGAINST OBESITY?

People who are obese or nearly obese can be sensitive to what they may interpret as the company monitoring their lifestyle. Some may even believe incorrectly that there are laws to prevent discrimination against overweight people in the workplace. In fact, the legal protection is narrow. At the beginning of 2009, Michigan was the only state, along with the District of Columbia, with a law prohibiting discrimination based on weight.[10]

However, instituting a policy of charging obese employees a higher premium does raise a number of procedural questions, says Janice Bellace, a professor of legal studies and business ethics at The Wharton School of the University of Pennsylvania, such as: "Do you have regular weigh-ins? And who qualifies as obese? If you strictly follow the body mass index (BMI) criteria, even people with a BMI of 25 or 26 are considered overweight."

The obesity epidemic presents a dilemma, according to Bellace, because although companies want their employees to lose weight, "they don't want to fire people for being overweight, or even refuse to hire them, because two-thirds of Americans are overweight."

FIGHT FAIR AGAINST SMOKING

If you're considering a policy of penalizing employees who smoke, you're more likely to be perceived as fair if you also do something to help them quit. To get started, the American Cancer Society (http://www.cancer.org) offers a model policy called "Smoking in the Workplace" that establishes a procedure for setting up a tobacco-free work environment. And the American Lung Association (http://www.lungusa.org) offers a range of services on implementing a smoke-free policy, including free consultation to management teams, unions, and employees on proper steps each must take toward a smoke-free goal.

How can you help your smoking employees quit? The Surgeon General advises a comprehensive program that combines insurance coverage for medication and even counseling.

The Professional Assisted Cessation Therapy (PACT) consortium has published a blueprint, *Employers' Smoking Cessation Guide: Practical Approaches to a Costly Workplace Problem*, which is available at http://www.endsmoking.org. The PACT guide recommends that, as an employer, you:

- Provide employees with self-help materials such kick-the-habit brochures.
- Look into the various types of telephone-based counseling offered by states, pharmaceutical companies, health promotion service providers, or by your own health plan.
- Offer subsidized access to online counseling services and information.
- Check with your Employee Assistance Program to see if it provides smoking-cessation counseling.
- Develop a policy that allows your employees to take part in programs during breaks or during working hours.
- Take an integrated approach to policies, health plans, and workplace programs for maximum impact.

America's Health Insurance Plans (AHIP) and the Kaiser Permanente Center for Health Research offer an online ROI calculator to find the potential return on investment of cessation programs (http://www.businesscaseroi.org/). Interventions to reduce smoking yield a positive return on investment within just a couple years for health plans and immediate savings for employers, according to the AHIP/Kaiser research. Using the ROI calculator, researchers found that health plans investing $35 to $410 per participant in a one-year program generated a positive ROI within two years.

If you choose to offer a smoking cession program, you're in good company. A third of companies with more than 200 employees offer programs, according to a Kaiser Family Foundation survey. Among smaller firms, the foundation finds that it's 1 in 12 companies.

United Parcel Service began offering its smoking cessation program in 2007 to the estimated 13 percent of its employees who use tobacco. The Union Pacific railroad credits its smoking cessation program with helping cut the smoking rate of its 50,000-plus workforce to about 17 percent, compared with 40 percent in the 1990s.[11]

THE BIG STICK

A few companies take a very aggressive stance against smoking. They fire workers who use tobacco, even off the job, and refuse to hire job applicants who smoke. So far, the results have included lawsuits and legislation to protect workers from being fired for legal activities that take place off the job.

Weyco, the Michigan-based benefits management company, has received much attention since 2005 when it fired four workers who did not quit smoking. The company had given employees 15 months to quit before beginning random nicotine testing.

In 2007 Scotts Miracle-Gro began screening out job candidates who use tobacco and announced it would conduct random tests for nicotine. At least one worker has sued the Ohio-based lawn and garden company.

By 2007, thirty-two state statutes restricted what companies may prohibit, according to the Littler law firm report *Employer Mandated Wellness Initiatives: Restricting Workplace Rights While Controlling Health Care Costs* (http://www.littler.com/presspublications, p. 15).

A company risks hurting itself with a no-smokers policy because "occasionally you have to turn down the best applicant" if that person is a smoker, says Lewis Maltby, president of the National Work-rights Institute in Princeton, New Jersey. Given the estimated percentage of smokers in the overall population, 20 percent of time you're going to turn down your top choice, he claims. That means you have to weigh the cost of health-care savings against sometimes hiring the second-best person for the job.[12]

Firing or refusing to hire smokers may be an unnecessarily aggressive approach. Employees are much more likely to see it as fair and reasonable to make smokers pay higher premiums because they incur higher health-care costs.

Encouraging employees is fine, says Michael Carter of the Hay Group, but he strongly advises against attempts to control them. "Employees are controlled enough as it is. If you want your program to be successful, employees have to believe it is reasonable and fair," he says. A controlling approach "might save money on health care, but we might end up having higher turnover. You need to look at the big picture."

LEGAL RISK ASSESSMENT

But mandates may be the way of the future. San Francisco attorney Garry G. Mathiason of Littler Mendelson, P.C., foresees a day when employees will be required to avoid unhealthy habits to get insurance or to keep a job. "Seat belts is a good analogy," he says, citing the slow evolution from studies that proved their efficacy to laws requiring their use. "The workplace is following the same path."[13]

If your organization chooses a mandatory approach—one that requires employees to participate and imposes some penalty if they don't—make sure you run the plan past your attorney to avoid possible conflicts with federal and state laws, especially those covering discrimination.

One notable example is the Health Insurance Portability and Accountability Act (HIPAA), which has specific but workable requirements for health plans covered by the Employee Retirement Income Security Act (ERISA), which is most employer health plans. HIPAA says that ERISA-covered plans may not discriminate based on a health factor. The list of factors includes medical condition, claims experience, receipt of health care, and, more generally, medical history and health status. Nicotine addiction is a health factor covered by the HIPAA nondiscrimination rules. So is body mass index, notably with regard to obesity.

However, the easiest way to avoid health-factor conflict with HIPAA is to focus your wellness program on *participation* rather than results. As long as your program does not provide a reward tied to a health factor, it does not discriminate based on that health factor. So, an incentive given for taking part in a wellness activity, rather than achieving a particular target or standard, generally is not discriminatory under HIPAA.

The risk of discrimination does exist with wellness incentives, but "much more can be done [by employers] than previously assumed," says Garry Mathiason. He was lead author of the report *Employer Mandated Wellness Initiatives: Respecting Workplace Rights While Controlling Health Care Costs* (http://www.littler.com/presspublications), which lists types of incentives that are based on participation rather than results:

- A program that reimburses the cost of membership in a health center.
- A program that rewards employees for attending monthly health education seminars.
- An incentive to participate in a cholesterol, blood pressure, or other screening program that is paid regardless of outcome.
- Reimbursement for weight loss and smoking cessation programs paid regardless of outcome.

What makes such wellness incentives legal and acceptable has nothing to do with an employee's health status. It has to do with what an employee is willing to do to improve his or her own health.

CHALK LINES

Wellness planners received clarification about HIPAA when the Labor Department's Employee Benefits Security Administration (EBSA), the Department of Health and Human Services, and the Internal Revenue Service issued final federal regulations relating to wellness programs.

The regulations, which apply to voluntary and mandatory wellness plans beginning on or after July 1, 2007, don't make it any easier to offer incentives, but they do encourage plan sponsors to think through what they're trying to accomplish, instead of jumping on the bandwagon. When they get into what the regulations say and impose, the immediate reaction is: Why are we really doing this? What are our goals? Can we do it? They still can, but now there are borders to play by.

"The analogy I use is football," says Fritz Hewlett, a vice president with Aon Consulting's Health and Benefits practice. "What they've done is put chalk lines down so we know where the end of the field is, where the yard lines are. A structure has been added, making it clearer."

The regulations say that to be nondiscriminatory, wellness programs that provide a reward must meet certain requirements:

1. The total reward to an individual cannot exceed 20 percent of the total cost of employee-only coverage.
2. The program must be "reasonably" designed to promote health or prevent disease.
3. Eligible individuals must have the opportunity to qualify for the reward at least once per year.
4. The program must be available to all "similarly situated individuals," with a reasonable alternative standard for people whose medical conditions would make attaining the standard unreasonably difficult or medically inadvisable, as attested by the participant's personal physician.
5. All program materials must disclose the availability of the reasonable alternative standard or the possibility of waiver of the standard.[14]

These regulations can help clear up a number of key questions. For example, can you offer a nonsmoker a discount on his/her health premium? The answer is yes, but to do so in accordance with HIPAA, the discount must be uniformly available. That means you also must offer an alternative way to receive the discount, such as by taking part in a smoking cessation program.

The final regulations make it very clear, says Hewlett. "Even if you have an individual who is a smoker and on the surface would not qualify for a non-smoker discount, if the smoker participates in the program that person is eligible."

What if you want to give people a reward for participating in a health risk assessment? (See chapter 6 for more on health assessment.) Yes, you can do it, Hewlett says. "HIPAA doesn't impact that. You're not rewarding the attainment of a particular health standard," because it's the participation in the assessment, not the results of the assessment, that matters.

EBSA released a checklist that addresses what types of programs must comply with the final program regulations. It can help you determine whether your program is in compliance. (See Appendix C.)

OTHER LEGAL CONCERNS

HIPAA is not the only legal concern regarding wellness incentives. You also must consider the Americans with Disabilities Act (ADA), which has its own antidiscrimination safeguards, particularly with regard to employee benefits.

According to the Littler law firm report, ADA will certainly apply "if an employee is able to perform the essential functions of his or her job but, because of a disability, is unable to achieve a health factor requirement under a mandatory wellness plan."

ADA also imposes strict confidentiality rules about disclosure of medical information. While the Equal Employment Opportunities Commission has taken the position that it is permissible to ask for personal health data as part of a voluntary wellness program that focuses on early detection, screening, and management of disease, the ADA limits the circumstances under which an employer may ask questions about an employee's health or require the employee to have a medical examination.

The Age Discrimination in Employment Act (ADEA) is another concern, but it does permit a mandatory wellness program if it can be crafted to correspond to the reasonable expectations of the older worker. If a program requires an employee to achieve a certain health standard, that standard must take into account and even be adjusted for the age of the employee. Littler notes, for example, "Programs can mandate participation in an exercise or fitness program without requiring that everyone be able to run a certain distance at a certain speed."

In addition to age, "some of the classes protected by U.S. Title VII and similar state laws may be implicated in a mandatory wellness program. Gender and religion come to mind, but again, reasonable accommodation should lessen the risk of litigation," according to the Littler report.

Finally, keep in mind that a number of states have enacted laws that must be considered when designing a mandatory wellness program.

THE BOTTOM LINE

If you want employees to change their behavior, offer them meaningful incentives. If you want your incentive plan to be successful—and legal—give all employees a chance to take part and focus on participation rather than on outcomes. An incentive given for taking part in a wellness activity, rather than for achieving a particular target or standard, generally is not discriminatory under the Health Insurance Portability and Accountability Act (HIPAA).

You can offer many types of incentives: small prizes, chances at big prizes, points that can be accumulated for prizes, or cash prizes. But the prize that sends your message loudest and clearest is one that offers employees a rebate on their health insurance premiums when they take steps toward healthier behavior. Some organizations try disincentives, such as penalizing employees who smoke, but carrots work better than sticks and are more likely to be legal.

To make the most of your incentives plan, offer incentives to employees for taking a comprehensive health assessment. Chapter 6 explains the hows and whys of health assessments.

Profile: Lincoln Industries' Peak Performance (http://www.lincolnindustries.com)

At Lincoln Industries the carrot is a mountain. Mountain climbing is the incentive that the metal-finishing company offers only to employees who are in top physical form.

Lincoln Industries chose a mountain climb because it is a good analogy for the journey that individuals need to make for their own wellness—it requires setting high goals, building a plan, and celebrating at the peak, says Dan Krick, vice president, people resources.

The company, which employees more than 600 people in Lincoln, Nebraska, has a lot to celebrate. It has reaped a five-to-one total return on its wellness investment. While the manufacturing industry average for health-care costs per person is about $9,800, for Lincoln Industries, it is just over $4,200 per person. Workers compensation costs were more than $500,000 in 2003. Three years later, those costs had dropped to less than $50,000.

The company has been recognized as a Great Place to Work by the Society for Human Resource Management and the Great Place to Work Institute. It has received numerous awards for its wellness program, including the Department of Health and Human Services' "Innovation in Prevention" Award and the American Heart Association's Platinum Award for "Start! Fit-Friendly Workplace." It is a winner of the Wellness Council of America's (WELCOA) Platinum Award.

Fittingly enough, Lincoln Industries calls its wellness program "go! Platinum." Participation in various activities helps employees earn bronze, silver, gold, or platinum status. The rankings are based on seven criteria: tobacco use, quarterly checks (blood pressure, flexibility, body fat), participation in wellness events, health information update, health risk assessment, blood profile, behavior-based safety participation, and safe work behavior. Employees must participate in at least 75 percent of the wellness activities to attain platinum membership.

Each year, Lincoln Industries caps its wellness efforts with a trip to Colorado to climb a *Fourteener*—one of the state's dozens of mountains that rise more than 14,000 feet. The expeditions are open only to those who have attained the platinum level of fitness and not have smoked for at least six months.

"Only one percent of the U.S. population is fit enough to climb a mountain of that height. People climb on the company dollar and there's a celebration afterward. It's something that is quite rigorous," says Krick, who has taken part in several climbs—and celebrations.

Lincoln Industries arranged for its first mountain climb in 2004. Three years later, 84 people—more than 17 percent of the workforce—qualified for the climb of Mt. Quandary, outside of Breckenridge, Colorado. "It's amazing. People have given up lifelong habits to do this," Krick says, citing a forklift driver who said that he quit smoking after nine years because he wanted to be part of the expedition.[15]

The award-winning wellness program first got off the ground more than 15 years ago, when Lincoln Industries hired an on-site occupational nurse who did blood pressure screenings and handed out literature. It was a simple beginning, but it was the foundation of promoting the health of its workers.

About a decade ago, Lincoln Industries hired Tonya Vyhlidal as its full-time wellness and health-enhancement manager. Vyhlidal is part of the company's 12-person wellness committee, which develops ideas based on employee feedback and proposes them to senior management.

Resources are just as important as structure, according to Krick. "You may start small but you have to spend some money to get some money."

Not all of the programs are as elaborate—or as lofty—as a mountain trek. For example, the company promotes Wellness Wednesday with events such as a walk around the corporate campus. There are weight-management programs, bike rides, health education seminars, and yoga classes. Wellness mentors follow up after physicals, to help employees progress toward the seven goals. Lincoln Industries offers a fitness reimbursement program but doesn't have it's own fitness center.

The company offers the usual small rewards, but tee shirts or raffles get you only so far, Krick says. The company believes in integrating wellness into benefits and offering incentives that hit people in the pocketbook. Wellbucks is such a program. It's a cash incentive that employees can earn when they participate in selected activities. Wellbucks are earned monthly and paid out quarterly. Up to $40 worth of Wellbucks can apply to health insurance costs each quarter.

Lincoln Industries has integrated wellness into its performance management and compensation systems. Everyone gets quarterly health assessments that include blood pressure screening and body weight, body fat, and flexibility measurements. Each employee reviews the quarterly results with the wellness manager or occupational nurse and sets individual wellness objectives. These objectives influence everyone's merit increase.

For supervisors and higher-level employees, wellness is also tied in with compensation. Krick reports that one year, it cost him between $500 and $1,000 dollars for missing his wellness objective.[16]

The company bans smoking from its facilities. It offers on-site tobacco cessation classes at no cost both to employees and to their family members, and classes are taken while participants are on the clock. Since 2000, tobacco use has gone from 77 percent to 23 percent. The company's program is structured to comply with the Health Insurance Portability and Accountability Act (HIPAA). Based on the honor system, those who do not smoke receive discounts on their health insurance—singles receive a $25 per month discount, while families receive a $50 a month discount.

Awareness, then education, then intervention are necessary progressions toward wellness. That final step is the most costly, but it changes behavior. "We want a program that pulls rather than pushes. We have a mixture of both," Krick says. The company even takes time to talk with suppliers and customers—such as Harley Davidson—about the need for workplace wellness.

He finds that Lincoln Industries' approach to wellness tends to attract healthier job applicants. Potential employees "know about our program and know they can be rewarded for a lifestyle they already have. They know they can have lower health insurance costs by being active, and they find that attractive."

But Krick doesn't encourage other companies to dive head first into wellness. Take baby steps. Start slowly building a healthy culture, he says. "When we raise the bar, people are already with us. When we wrote our tobacco-free policy the managers were originally more moderate but the general population said 'you've got to make it zero tolerance.'"

Chapter Six

Take the Risk out of Health Assessments

The health-risk assessment or appraisal, often known as an HRA, is a powerful wellness tool that helps your organization identify and reduce costly health threats. The assessment usually consists of a questionnaire about personal lifestyle and about personal and family medical history. It may include a physical examination, with laboratory work such as a cholesterol-level test. These assessments generate health profiles—individual profiles for the participants themselves and a group profile that gives your organization an overall picture of the workforce's wellness.

But often people are reluctant to take part in health risk assessments, making participation rates too low to be of much value. One way to put people's minds at ease: Take out the *risk*.

Why even use the word *risk*? "It causes fear. People are afraid to know what the results are going to be," says Hewitt consultant Tim Stentiford. Employees tend to feel, "they're taking my blood but no one is giving me anything back . . . Employers bring risk and fear to the table. They don't bring support and hope."

Many organizations and vendors prefer the straightforward term *health assessment*, which alleviates the fear of discovering illness by focusing on wellness and well-being. You can make the assessment a positive event that not only has participants fill out questionnaires and take blood tests, but allows them time to meet with a health coach—or even a massage therapist. To encourage participation, add a little immediate gratification to the process.

And take a consumer marketing approach when promoting health assessments. Tell the story about the business reason to control health-care costs that makes this necessary for the company. "You can be more transparent and get more response from the people who are skeptical. If organizations were more honest about the story behind it, it would remove some of the barriers," says Stentiford.

WHO SEES THE DATA?

Employees who are reluctant to take health assessments aren't just worried about getting bad news about their health—often they're worried about invasions of their privacy. Everyone has heard stories of personal data that has been stolen, accidentally lost, or deliberately misused.

The National Workrights Institute goes so far as to warn workers that developments in science and technology are on a collision course with their rights. "New technologies and scientific developments are giving employers easy access to a multitude of information about their employees' health—and likely future medical expenses. This health-related information is finding its way into employment decisions in hiring, promotions and down-sizing," according to an institute statement.

Your company may have every intention of doing the right thing, but employers' general track record is not impressive when it comes to protecting confidential data. "Keeping employee information confidential never seems to be a high priority," says Lewis Maltby, the institute's president.

At some point no matter how much of a firewall is in place, employee privacy is threatened, believes Pam Dixon, executive director of the World Privacy Forum. "There is someone who knows who has chosen to participate in a [wellness] program" and who may not keep the information confidential.

To counter concerns, at the very beginning of the health assessment process make clear to employees that they have protection under the Health Insurance Portability and Accountability Act (HIPAA). Let them know that if they feel in any way compromised, they have legal remedies. You'll probably never get 100 percent of your employees convinced that their data is safe, but if you have developed an overall culture of trust and spell out the protections employees have, you are likely to have better participation in health assessments.

An accepted way to help protect employees' privacy is to use third-party vendors to do the assessments and to report back only aggregate information to the employer. When choosing a vendor, it can be a case of buyer beware, but the nonprofit National Committee for Quality Assurance is preparing a set of standards for companies that sell assessment products. Before you choose a vendor, ask questions to determine if the health assessment product has the technology and content needed to meet your specifications as defined by your objectives. For example, does the vendor include an option for sending reports to employees' physicians? Does it include individualized health education materials with participant reports? Does the data track assessment results over time? What's the level of level of customization available? And, of course, how good are the methods for preventing confidentiality breeches?[1]

Third-party administration of health assessments is seen a step in the right direction toward protecting individual privacy. But even when there's a third party, "there has to be a contact point when [the assessment is] tied to any reward at all. It doesn't mean that they are going to get your medical history, but they know you did something in a wellness program. That's problematic for employees," Dixon says. She sees employee privacy as an area ripe for greater transparency and oversight and predicts that eventually there will be a lot of legislation on the subject.

While each individual receives his/her health report from the vendor, the company receives only a group profile. The goal is to identify high areas of risk, such as what percentage of the group is not up to date with relevant screenings and immunizations.

When providing the aggregate information to a client, the vendor tries "to see what's off kilter" in the overall picture and recommend ways to fix it, says Mike Casey, senior director for population health management at Mayo Clinic Health Solutions. "We try to provide not just data, but consultation as well and recommendations of what you might do. When you do a consultation year after year you can look at the impact over time."

Determining who presents health assessment results and the level of follow-up employees receive will vary based on your objectives. You might choose to have the results presented by health professionals who are provided by the vendor or contractor or by health-plan employees. Or you may be able to use specially trained staff members. The follow-up itself can range from feedback only to referrals for individual counseling for high-risk employees or those with chronic conditions.[2]

Needles and Pens

Before starting down the health-assessment path, make sure you are clear about your objectives, about how you plan to administer the assessment itself, and how you will communicate results to employees. (See Appendix D.)

The process usually is part paper and pen (or computer screen) and part needles and lab tests. It should not rely only on individuals reporting about their own health; one wellness expert dryly notes that when questioned, some people suddenly become a few inches taller and a few pounds lighter.

The questionnaire itself need not, and probably should not, be lengthy. It generally should cover such topics as exercise, diet, and sleep habits; tobacco and alcohol use; and stress; medications; vaccinations; dental care; and how illness and other factors have affected productivity and time off from work. The questionnaire also should cover behavior concerning safety, such as seat belt use.

Dr. D. W. Edington, director of the University of Michigan's Health Management Research Center, has spent more than 25 years studying how individual health promotion, worksite wellness activities, and programs within organizations affect health-care cost containment and productivity. His philosophy is to keep assessments short and simple, perhaps no more than 55 questions.

Some companies prefer paper questionnaires; others do everything online. Mayo Clinic Health Solutions clients do all assessments online, for example, Mike Casey says, because "we've looked at the trends and we've seen the paper version going away." The advantage is that an online version can be more tailored and a little less expensive than a paper version.

In some industries, employees don't have easy access to computers, however. That's why Navistar International Corporation, which produces international commercial trucks with a workforce of 18,000, offers both online and paper questionnaires.

At the WELCOA Platinum award winner, "it's probably 50–50," with the blue-collar population relying on paper questionnaires, says Dr. William Bunn, vice president of health, safety, security, and productivity.

The questionnaire takes about 10 to 12 minutes. The longer a health assessment is, the more probable it is that they won't take it, but that could be influenced by incentives, Bunn says. "We could probably do a longer one now that we give money"—a $200 discount per employee on their health-care premium—for taking part in the assessment.

Over the years, Navistar has tried different assessments and now uses one offered by the University of Michigan Health Management Research Center.

There's no magic bullet, no one assessment product that works for everyone. You have to look at the assessment and make sure you've got one that matches your population. Keep in mind that if you switch, you have to start over because different vendors use different questions.

It's difficult to determine Navistar's return on investment, Bunn admits. "We know that it helps. People who take [assessments] are cheaper and they stay cheaper, but how much is hard to figure out. We believe we get back the cost of the assessment and an additional increment on top of that."

Navistar has begun using incentives to encourage family members to take part in the assessment process. Covering family members as well as employees is a great idea. But less than 20 percent of organizations reach out to family members, estimates Tim Stentiford of Hewitt, because it's harder to administer the assessment to off-site individuals.

While it may be harder reach the entire family, doing so not only helps family members improve their health, but "it can improve trust and mitigate the Big Brother concern. The employee is more likely to feel the employer is telling me the honest story when it is now reaching out to my family," says Stentiford. Also, "the person at home is often the influencer, the decision maker. If you market it to the home, you might get higher traction."

NOT JUST QUESTIONS

For the more than 5,000 employees (plus spouses) of Community Medical Centers in the Fresno, California, area, the annual health questionnaire only takes 10 to 15 minutes, but that certainly doesn't mean the process is finished. Community Medical Centers found that too many of the people who completed the questionnaire part of the assessment did not proceed any further with lab work, biometrics (the statistical analysis of biological phenomena), and coaching sessions. So now, employees are not defined as *enrolled* until they have completed all of these four components. An individual's assessment is not considered in the aggregate reporting until both

PROVIDING THE BEST FEEDBACK

To ensure a continuous dialogue and foster effective behavior change, it is important that not too much time elapse between the first contact, the assessment, and a follow-up. Best practices support immediate feedback to employees as well as to employers. The same day that the assessment is completed, participants can have a written report as well as recommendations for health improvement.

But if immediate results are not feasible, results within two weeks are acceptable. Employees respond best to personalized reports outlining their risks and the resources available to them for improving their health. Employers with access to aggregate reports and/or executive summaries can begin to understand the overall health of their populations, track risks, and monitor programs.

Experts recommend the use of risk scores in feedback to help employees gauge their relative risks as well as increase their motivation to improve or maintain their health status.

What are the different methods of follow-up to an assessment? Employees should always be granted the option of being contacted after an assessment. Once a risk factor is identified and the employee has given his or her consent to be contacted, a variety or a combination of different follow-up methods can be used.

Popular follow-up methods used by National Business Group on Health members include the following:

- Health coach contact; telephonic (recommended for first contact), electronic, or in person
- Electronic personalized materials or links to resources
- 24-hour nurse line
- Tear-off sheet to take to the employee's physician
- Review with personal wellness coordinator
- Follow-up with occupational health nurses/health professionals at the worksite
- Immediate one-on-one counseling by subject-matter expert/health professional

> Offering several different options for employee follow-up allows the greatest chance of achieving high satisfaction as well as removing potential barriers to compliance. Not every individual will prefer the same method of follow-up, and reports indicate that when information and resources are convenient for people to access, they are more likely to use them.
>
> It's been reported that one-on-one counseling sessions achieve the greatest employee satisfaction levels, and they are highly recommended for initial contacts. Once the employee has been contacted, the contacting party can ask how the employee prefers to be reached in the future.
>
> Adapted from the National Business Group on Health. "Health Risk Assessment Toolkit: A Road Map for Employers" 2007.

lab results and biometrics are entered, and results are not entered until the employee meet's with a wellness coach.

Questionnaires alone are not enough, says Rex A. Wilcox, manager for the centers' C-Fit Community Wellness Program. "The downside is that self reporting is not always reliable. We wanted to make sure we had hard data that could be measurable from year to year."

So, when a person completes the questionnaire, he or she receives a lab coupon. Whether the process progresses is in his/her hands. Community Medical Centers makes the process as easy as possible by offering the free tests in its own hospital labs. Those who do not complete their labs within 90 days of their assessment are asked to retake the assessment to ensure that centers have the most accurate, up-to-date health information, Wilcox says.

Results of the tests are only seen on the administrative end by the assigned wellness coach, who sets up an appointment to discuss the results with the participant. Participants can meet with their coach up to four times a year.

When the process is complete, participants receive gift cards worth $75 that are redeemable at local retail stores, and those who are in the company PPO are eligible to receive a $150 premium reduction.

When is the best time to schedule health assessments? Merely sending out information on healthy behaviors and asking employees to take the initiative is not nearly as effective as linking assessments to open enrollment periods. Open enrollment marks the one time of the year when employees' attention is focused on their benefits programs, notes Jeri Stepman, Watson Wyatt Worldwide's national leader for health and welfare administration.

Fifty-three percent of company representatives surveyed by Watson Wyatt said they incorporated health assessments into their enrollment systems or planned to incorporate these programs in the near future. Thirty-six percent said they already use enrollment systems to encourage employees to sign up for disease management programs, or planned to do so soon. "Including behavior-change information and decision-support tools directly in the enrollment process can make a big difference in the number of people who sign up for wellness programs and take them seriously," Stepman says.

TO MANDATE OR NOT TO MANDATE?

The World Privacy Forum argues that health assessments should never be mandatory. But a growing number of companies think otherwise. Some experts are beginning to see assessments as the price of entry into the health-care system.

Obviously, making it mandatory gets you the highest participation, but there can be a backlash, with people feeling forced. If a company does not have a culture of trust, a mandatory approach may be perceived as coercion, and the entire wellness program may be seen as part of the enemy to be resisted.

How well mandatory assessments succeed depends on how they are portrayed and how well employees are prepared for this step. The process should be thoughtfully introduced over time so that employees come to see it as just part of what they do when enrolling in the health plan. For example, some employers continue to offer a choice of plans, but participating in the assessment allows the employee to be part of a more desirable health plan. Those who do not participate have another, traditional, health plan they can opt into. If there is basic trust and the approach is carefully communicated and thoughtfully implemented, integrating the health assessment into your overall health plan has the potential to provide a rich, reliable database.

In 2005 when Cadmus Communications Corp., a publishing company in Richmond, Virginia, began requiring each worker to take a health assessment to qualify for medical coverage, some employees expressed fear that their medical conditions could cost them their jobs. Although employees were assured the results would be made available only to Cadmus's health insurer, CIGNA Corp., and wouldn't lead to punitive measures, 17 workers decided to drop coverage rather than comply, *The Wall Street Journal* reported.

The program may be controversial, but Cadmus saw a 21 percent drop in hospital admissions, a 44 percent reduction in the length of hospital stays, and a 33 percent decrease in diagnostic testing costs in one year.[3]

CIGNA instituted a similar program for its employees after seeing the results at Cadmus. The program started out as voluntary, with a modest incentive, and participation was only lukewarm. CIGNA decided to make assessments mandatory when it introduced its Healthy Life program. The goal is to keep all wellness-related activities under one umbrella. Health assessments became a core piece of the program because the company felt it needed to get a baseline.

CIGNA rolled out the program in fall 2005, making it part of the 2006 annual enrollment. If an employee wanted medical coverage for 2006, he or she was required to complete a health assessment. "If you didn't, you wouldn't have any medical coverage," says Marilyn Paluba, who oversees CIGNA employee benefit. "We took advantage of benefits enrollment to get everybody's attention. People went to meetings to learn about their benefits and there were sections of meetings" about health assessments.

In 2008 CIGNA extended health assessments to spouses and partners who enrolled in medical coverage. At the same time, the company added some basic laboratory work, such as cholesterol level testing. "We told people up front why we were doing it, that our focus [as a company] is on health and we need to have healthy practices ourselves. We told them this was a resource, a tool to develop their own personal health plan," Paluba says. Any organization faces resistance to change. "There are always a few people who are concerned. You have to be up front with people; people will ask questions. They want to know 'What are you going to do with the data?' We tell them 'it's yours.' When people understood that [the information] was theirs, most people were on board, from the top down."

Paluba is careful to explain to employees that the company only receives high-level summary information, that it uses that information to make the overall wellness program more responsive to people's needs. "We said these things are what you told us are most important to you: physical activity, weight management, nutrition, work/life balance, following through on fitness."

Good communication and strong support from top management, including the CEO, was critical to the success of CIGNA's Healthy Life program. The company has kept its focus on the benefits of health assessments and wellness, rather than going on the defensive, she says. "We said that as an employer we're willing to step up to the plate. We know how important it is to your health. When we started it, we linked it to prevention. We cover preventive care at 100 percent. We're saying that we think it's so important that we're going to pay the cost of it."

More companies are beginning to see wellness programs and preventive care as a way of controlling health costs in a way that is really benefiting individuals. The message, Paluba says, is not about shifting costs, "it's about making people healthier. We call this an investment. We're investing in people's health and well-being."

CARROTS OR STICKS REDUX

Wellness experts prefer carrots to sticks. Instead of *requiring* employees to take assessments, experts more often recommend offering incentives to those who voluntarily agree to do so. (See chapter 5.)

Often companies find the assessment participation rate is too low, says Dr. D. W. Edington, of the University of Michigan's Health Management Research Center, and so "the mathematics are not there. You need 90 percent participation and most get about 30 to 40 percent. Incentives drive the participation rate."

Many companies, especially large ones, do offer incentives. *The Wall Street Journal* has reported on several:

- Employees of Molson Coors Brewing Co.'s U.S. unit who fill out an assessment form and follow up on any medical advice receive a $200 discount on their annual health-care premiums.

- U.S. employees of the pharmaceutical giant AstraZeneca PLC who undergo an annual health assessment receive a $50 monthly discount on their health-insurance premiums.

- Dell Inc. gives a $75 deduction from their annual health-care premium to employees who agree to a health assessment, and those who complete a wellness program for managing health risks get an extra $225 deposited into an account that reimburses employees for medical expenses.

If you decide on the carrot approach, the best advice is to start simply. The first time an employee participates in an assessment, give the person a book about wellness. Then bump it up a notch and give a gift card. Then integrate health assessments into the health plan so that those who complete an assessment get a break on their premium or pay a lower deductible.

The logic is that the employee is taking some responsibility for better understanding his/her health, which will cost the employer less, "so we want to share some of that with you," says David R. Anderson, senior vice president, chief health officer and a cofounder of StayWell Health Management. While still an incentive-based strategy, "this approach is much less costly to the employer than cash incentives, has tax advantages, and is a step toward integrating health action into the very fabric of the organization and culture," he says.

Whatever you decide, plan carefully. Realize that the real long-range goal is to change the culture, so that you don't have worry about using gimmicks to get people to participate.

ASSESSING PRODUCTIVITY

The most enlightened employers realize that productivity costs are three to four times greater than health-care costs and they are moving beyond the basic health assessment to try to tease out the impact health has on productivity. There are several types of productivity-screening tools that can be used in conjunction with health assessments. Two of the most well-regarded are discussed below.

The Work Limitations Questionnaire (WLQ) measures the degree health problems interfere with an individual's ability to perform job tasks. The scores quantify productivity loss in terms of time management, mental/interpersonal, output, and physical demands of the job. The WLQ was developed at the Health Institute of the Tufts-New England Medical Center by Dr. Debra Lerner and Dr. Benjamin C. Amick III.

The Health and Performance Questionnaire (HPQ) is designed to assess the impact of health on four aspects of work functioning: time missed from work, performance while at work, injuries or illnesses at work, and job turnover. It was developed by researchers at the Harvard Medical School Department of Health Care Policy under Ronald C. Kessler, Ph.D., professor of health-care policy, in collaboration with the World Health Organization (WHO).

WHEN THE DATA'S IN

Companies spend time, energy, and money getting people to take health and productivity assessments, but what happens with the data when it's been collected?

The company can use the summary information it receives to build programs that address specific risks. For example, based on the results of the assessments, an employer can decide whether it would be best to introduce healthier food choices in the cafeteria, to offer nutrition classes, to implement an exercise programs, or to open a fitness center. The employer usually has limited resources and so will want to maximize its bang for the buck. The health assessment can provide a treasure trove of relevant information.

Individuals can use the information they receive to make their own health improvements and should be encouraged to share the results of the health assessments with their primary care physician. But the health assessment should not be thought of as an intervention that will dramatically modify an individual's behavior or cure a disease. A health assessment is not likely to get a return on investment on a stand-alone basis. If companies are expecting one, they are not looking at the health assessment correctly. They should look at it as tool, albeit a very valuable key tool in the overall program.

While there is little evidence that the health assessment itself changes behavior meaningfully, "it helps in the change process. It's a springboard to the right program; it might help nudge a person in the early stages of the process, where the goal is just to get them thinking about changing a health behavior," says David Anderson.

Along with helping the participant think about change, the greatest value of the health assessment is as a triage tool that identifies the health behaviors that need the most improvement and — crucial for engagement—which ones the participant is open to working on.

Measuring factors such as alcohol use, tobacco use, or obesity is relatively easy. The next, more sensitive level, is measuring readiness to change. For example, one year a person might be at risk due to being overweight, but not at all ready to address the issue. But if the company does a good job of education about the risks of obesity, in the second year that person might still be at risk but ready to deal with the problem.

The education message needs to be tailored to each person's inclination to change, so that if the person is not convinced, you give them more education, more moving down the path. When someone is ready to change, it's time to direct the person into a program that addresses the issues.

The assessment is the catalyst but you must have follow-up intervention. "You may have woke the individual up a little, but how do you take advantage of that? You need follow-up programs, such as online, telephonic or onsite coaching to get people to engage," says Mike Casey of Mayo Clinic Health Solutions. "The critical mistake is to look at the assessment as the be-all and end-all of the program. You need to channel people" into the programs that will best help them to maintain their health.

Over time, you will be able to measure change at the population level and see if your wellness program is moving forward.

AMBASSADOR PROGRAM

With a little more effort and resources you may be able to turn your assessment process into a larger kind of outreach program in which employees help others and form healthier communities.

For example, companies often target female employees who aren't getting mammograms, but what Tim Stentiford of Hewitt believes should be done is to is target the women who *are* getting the procedure. Learn what barriers stood in the way of their getting mammograms and how they overcame those barriers. Then enlist them as ambassadors.

Give these ambassadors coupons good for one free mammogram, paid for by the company, Stentiford urges. "They can give it to someone at work, at church. It's getting people to do the right thing in a sustained way. It really is that simple. That will take the compliance rate to near 100 percent."

Not only will an ambassador program improve your workers' health, but "it is also is a great story to tell to employees and families and communities: We are going to be leaders. We're going to be trend setters. We're going to motivate people," he says. That way the health assessment gets transformed into building a culture "where companies say this is right thing to do. And we're going to do it the right way. It's everyone's business to take care of each other."

THE BOTTOM LINE

Heath assessments are a great way to identify the top health risks in your organization, but you have to get employees to take them. To convince them to take part in the assessment progress, show them how you are protecting their privacy and offer them some type of incentive, preferably tied to their insurance premiums. You can require that employees take assessments, but the carrot is mightier than the stick.

The health assessment process is not just a matter of having employees fill out questionnaires. Include lab work and biometrics (the statistical analysis of biological phenomena), and follow-up with coaching sessions.

Set your expectations at the right level. A health assessment is a catalyst for a behavior change program, it's not a behavior change program of itself. Use the information you receive from assessments to build a stronger wellness program that addresses the specific risks your organization faces. To help more effectively combat those risks, you might consider an on-site medical clinic and/or fitness center. For information about setting up and running on-site facilities, see chapter 7.

Profile: Miles Ahead in the Health Assessment Process (http:www.mileskimball.com)

Miles Kimball Company is miles ahead of many companies in the health assessment process. The company, based in Oshkosh, Wisconsin, introduced voluntary health assessments when it launched its wellness program in 2001. Incentives initially were based on participation in wellness events but now are based on biometric results. Assessments are now mandatory for employees and spouses who receive health insurance through the company.

The annual assessment includes cholesterol and blood glucose tests and blood pressure, body mass index, and body fat screening. Each individual also completes a questionnaire, online or on paper, about physical activity, stress, smoking, alcohol and drug use, and existing medical conditions such as heart disease, cancer, diabetes, stroke, chronic bronchitis, or emphysema.

The process only takes about 10 minutes. It's done on company time and goes pretty quickly. But it hasn't always gone smoothly. Employees' privacy was a huge concern when the company started making the assessment mandatory in 2004. "A couple of people stood up at meetings and said 'You don't have the right to do this,'" says Susan Boettcher, human resource manager for the catalog company. "We're said we're paying 70 percent of your health insurance, we spend more than a million dollars a year for you and your family." With discussion, people came to understand the need for reducing health costs through the wellness program costs, she says, and accepted assurances that their privacy would be protected.

At Miles Kimball, the occupational health nurse does receive each individual's data, but she has a patient/nurse relationship so that what she learns she does not share with the employer. "I can't pinpoint individual results, nor do I want to. I want the big picture, to be able to say that as a group, this is how we're doing," says Boettcher, who believes that trust in an organization's motives has to be built up over time. Starting with a voluntary program gave employees a better understanding of how the process works and reduced resistance to the idea.

POINT SYSTEM

When the program began, employees could receive points on their health scorecard simply by participating in wellness events. Today, the scorecard, and the financial incentives, are based on biometrics, on the measuring and analyzing of biological data.

The scorecard is not pass / fail. It's a range of points on a 100-point scale. Cash incentives can be earned to help pay for future benefit premium costs based on the overall results. Participants who score between 89 and 100 points receive $30 per pay period/$720 per year to help pay for benefit costs; those who score between 70 and 88 points receive $15 per pay period. If a participant scores less than 70 points, the person doesn't receive anything for that benefits year.

Plus, employees who participate in the health assessment are eligible for an annual reimbursement of 50 percent of the cost of a health club membership, fitness program, or nutrition program, for a maximum of $50 reimbursement per year.

Participants who want to increase their scores can voluntarily meet with the occupational health nurse, who acts as a health coach. For example, if an employee is unable to keep her cholesterol level down by diet alone, the occupational health nurse will determine what is the best next step, such as getting in touch with the participant's physician.

The nurse might recommend something like an asthma clinic or a nutritional program, and if the person goes through the program, he or she can receive the monetary incentive. "It's at her discretion. If they are following the process, she has right to say you're doing everything you can, we will give you points. Or she can say once you follow program you can get the points," Boettcher says.

Plus, the assumption is if participants follow the program they will be able to score higher the following next year.

Miles Kimball now partners with Affinity Health System, which handles the company's health insurance, workers compensation and Employee Assistance Program. "We really wanted to bring it in under one roof so we could analyze the data. Affinity can go through our claims and give us the big picture. That way we can see where we have the greatest concerns in our population, and the wellness team can address them," she says. For example, the team can see what percentage of the participants are not getting recommended routine screenings and devise an educational program to address the problem.

Miles Kimball has been charting its return on investment since the program began in 2001. It has seen a 30 percent reduction in workers' comp costs and less than a 2.3 percent increase in health-care costs.

Boettcher is able to look at the overall health of the company based on risk factors. These factors are: body weight, physical activity, stress, cholesterol, blood pressure, smoking, alcohol, safety belt use, existing medical conditions, perceived health, life satisfaction, job satisfaction, illness days, health/age index, and zero risk management. Five or more risk factors puts participants in the high-risk category.

In 2001, 23 percent of the participants were ranked as low risk, 58 percent were ranked moderate risk, and 18 percent were high risk. In 2007, 63 percent were low risk, 25 were in the moderate risk category, and 12 percent were high risk. "To me, that says a lot. The people who are participating year after year are making changes," Boettcher says.

Obesity continues to be the number one area that people struggle with, and stress always ranks near the top. On the other hand, employees have been successful in reducing their cholesterol levels, and smoking has come down from about 20 to about 12 percent of the population.

"One of the things we love to see is that 18 percent of our population has zero risk. The people who are healthy, we try to keep them there," Boettcher says.

Las Vegas. Harrah's center is managed by Whole Health Management, an operator of corporate health and wellness facilities that manages similar centers for the company in Atlantic City, New Jersey; Lake Tahoe, California; New Orleans; and Tunica, Mississippi.

Each site is unique, designed to meet the needs of the different populations. Not surprisingly, Las Vegas is the largest. It has personal trainers, equipment, and room for classes such as yoga and core training. Nutritionists are available to everyone at no cost. When employees join, there's a tutorial on how machines work and how to sign up for personal training.

The center's mission is to help educate employees and keep them on track toward attaining their health goals, says Shana Wiley, Harrah's manager of benefits. The fitness center "is to encourage those who weren't going to the gym. We wanted to make it more convenient for our employees to learn about exercise."[6]

The center is an especially useful benefit for the many Harrah's employees who are new to the Las Vegas area, says spokesperson Jacqueline Peterson. "When you come into a new place, where do you go to the doctor, where do you go to the gym? It takes time to research. This is a great timesaver."

TRAINERS AND VENDORS

Having a staff of trainers or instructors on-site is a great value, but, if the budget is limited, it may not be required. Consultant Stephen Tharrett recommends having at least one full-time trainer who can lead orientations, perform assessments, and provide group instruction and overall supervision. And Tharrett tends "to be a fan of having the fitness center person be an employee. This creates greater alignment with the company values and goals. It also connects them directly to the HR or medical department."

The basic qualifications for a trainer are a college degree in the health/fitness arena and certification from a nationally recognized and accredited certification organization such as the National Organization for Competency Assurance (NOCA). The top certification groups are the American College of Sports Medicine (ACSM), the National Sports and Conditioning Association (NSCA), and the American Council on Exercise (ACE).

Many organizations, large and small, use outside companies to manage their centers. When using an independent contractor make sure you verify qualifications and establish a well written agreement with expectations spelled out. And make sure the contractor provides all the proper evidence of insurance coverage.

For Google contractor Plus One, managing a fitness center is part of the core business, something that isn't the case for most companies, Maraday notes. Operating a fitness center "is a serious delivery system—people can get hurt," he says. And while it make seem less expensive, at first glance, to manage one in house, he argues that outsourcing the fitness center improves the return on investment. When it's outsourced, fitness center use tends to be much higher because a vendor has the necessary promotional systems to attract participants.

In addition to proper equipment and effective promotion, any fitness center needs to have a general liability package that covers incidents in the center. Also, if there are professional staff members, they should have liability insurance. It should also be a requirement that all employees who use the facility complete a preactivity screening and sign a waiver/release. (For a sample waiver form, see Appendix E.)

Remember that a thorough orientation program can help you avoid employee injuries and employer liability problems. Leake, a clinical exercise specialist as well as program coordinator at Mercy Preventive Health Center, says a client company tried a new orientation approach—making a streaming video which could be put on the intranet employee Web site.

"We spent a week filming, giving a virtual tour of the facility, outlining the gym hours, rules and regulations, providing a hotline number to call with questions and a FAQ sheet on the website," he says. "We also provided a hands-on tour with instructors to go over any nuances and provide a greater learning experience. The orientation film has gone well, in that most employees did not have time to attend an orientation session."

One more suggestion for maximizing the impact of a corporate fitness center: make sure that the center conserves energy and uses eco-friendly products. That could mean using self-powered exercise equipment that reduces the need for electricity, or installing flooring and lockers made of recycled materials. It might also mean taking advantage of natural light and incorporating a rooftop garden to improve air quality. Maintaining a fitness center that takes into account the health of the environment as well as the health of employees is a great way to improve overall morale and productivity.

CONVENIENT, COST-SAVING CLINICS

A growing number of companies are proving some type of on-site medical care to employees. These on-site centers offer companies the opportunity to provide convenient access to care, lower their health-care costs, ensure a safer workplace, and achieve a competitive advantage through a healthier workforce, according to Watson Wyatt Worldwide's "2007/2008 Onsite Health Center Survey."

Perhaps that explains the findings of another Watson Wyatt study, this one conducted with the National Business Group on Health: The number of on-site health centers is growing. Nearly one-third of companies (29%) have or planned to have an on-site health-care center by 2009, up from 27 percent in 2006.[7]

Companies' motivations for setting up on-site health centers have changed over the years. They were first introduced to address occupational health and safety needs, but today they aim to reduce health-care costs and improve productivity. Asked about the main factors that motivated companies to adopt on-site health-care centers, employers cited improved worker productivity as first, according to the *Onsite Health Center Survey*. Reducing health-care costs, improving access to care, and addressing occupational health and safety needs were cited as other important factors.

Many employers integrate their clinics with their wellness programs, offering disease management, lifestyle behavior change, and coaching services. The most commonly available services at clinics tend to be preventive-care services, such as screenings and immunizations.

Ninety-six percent of the employers that took part in the *Onsite Health Center Survey* said they make on-site health center services available to employees who are enrolled in their health plan, and 71 percent of the employers said they provide services to part-time employees, even those who are not eligible to participate in the health plan.

Forty-four percent of the employers said they provide services to temporary workers, and 25 percent said they offer services to contract workers. Twenty-five percent of the employers surveyed said the clinic services are available to covered dependents, while 20 percent said retirees are offered access.

The past five years have seen an increase in the number of organizations that really understand the role of on-site centers in improving and maintaining employee health, says Patricia Berger-Friedman, a Watson Wyatt senior consultant for health-care strategy. After being "out of favor for a fairly long time . . . it's an exciting time for this type of activity," says Berger-Friedman. She sees particularly strong growth in white-collar industries such as finance and pharmaceuticals, where the on-site clinics keep highly skilled employees on the job instead of traveling to doctors' offices and sitting in waiting rooms.

IF YOU BUILD IT, WILL THEY COME?

Most on-site health-care centers can expect a three-to-one return on their investment within three years estimates Stuart Clark, executive vice president of Comprehensive Health Services (CHS) in Reston, Virginia. Obviously, increased employee attendance at on-site clinics helps boost that return.[8]

But workers at some companies have expressed worries that on-site health care violates their privacy because the same health providers taking care of their private medical needs also are in charge of treating them for work-related injuries on behalf of the company. Caregivers are too professional to violate a patient's privacy, Clark says, but employees can still be uneasy about it. "When employees are going to a clinic on their employer's property, the immediate question is 'Wait a minute. Where is this information going?'"

Take steps to explain to employees that the company receives only aggregate data, not individual records. "It requires a fair amount of messaging and assurances. It needs to be woven into the brand that 'my employer cares about me' and can be trusted," Clark says.

It's best to look at the clinic from the employee/consumers' point of view: What is the value proposition? Is the service convenient? Do they believe they are getting a high level of care? "It's got to be better than what they are currently receiving," says Gary Pritts, president of Eagle Consulting Partners in Cleveland. "When Jane Does goes to the on-site clinic, you want her to have a good experience and tell her co-workers," so that they will be motivated to make the switch too.

Ways to make the experience superior and to attract employees to the worksite clinic include allowing each patient more time with the caregiver or with health coaches, reduced copays, and one-time bonuses for going to the clinic.

Convenience is an important factor that affects whether an employee will use an on-site clinic. Is the location easily accessible to the majority of employees? Does the center have comprehensive operating hours? Does it offer the types of services employees need and want? The more services offered, the better the value proposition.

An on-site health center is a substantial financial commitment and one of the most highly visible aspects of a company's dedication to wellness. It requires physical space and medical equipment, plus trained staff. And it requires a certain critical mass to be cost effective. The more people who use the clinic, the more services it can offer, and the more attractive the clinic will be to employees and their families. If your company is too small to have a critical mass or has groups of employees scattered in many locations, it might be better to consider a clinic on wheels, a van with equipment and health-care providers that periodically takes services directly to employees.

How many are enough employees? A company can have a limited medical clinic with perhaps 500 employees, if spouses are included. Larger companies can have a minimal clinic offering primary care with pharmaceutical dispensing and staffed by a nurse practitioner with a part-time supervising physician, while the largest companies can offer clinics with such services as urgent care, wellness counseling, lifestyle coaching, physical therapy, and on-site pharmacy.

A dedicated on-site pharmacist working closely with a dedicated medical team can improve patient safety and bring a company great savings, because the pharmacist only has to deal with the company's own formulary, a book listing pharmaceutical substances along with their formulas, uses, and methods of preparation, says Dr. Raymond J. Fabius, strategic advisor to the president of Walgreen Health and Wellness division and former global medical leader at General Electric. "It's becoming clear to larger employers that [a pharmacy] is an important step to controlling costs and support higher levels of engagement and retention."

A full-scale clinic—one that offers acute care, preventive exams, and additional specialization, such as physical therapy or basic radiology—would require at least 2,500 to 3,000 employees to justify a front-end investment of roughly $3 million to $4 million, esti-mates David Beech, a health-care consultant with Watson Wyatt Worldwide.[9]

You can have just "a Band-Aid shop where people go to get patched up if they get nicks and bruises or have a stomach ache," says Jayne B. Lux, director of the Global Health Benefits Institute for the National Business Group on Health, or you can have a clinic that exemplifies the company's philosophy about health and well-being and is part of integrated health services.

If you do choose to invest in a clinic, think it through carefully. Is your population large enough to support it? What kinds of ser-vices do you want to offer? Will you include dependents as well as employees? How does it fit in with your overall wellness and orga-nizational priorities? There's no cookie-cutter approach that works for everyone. You'll need to find what works well enough for your company and for enough of your employees so that a clinic is cost effective.

PRACTICING MEDICINE

Must a health center have a physician on staff? The "perfect profile," according to Stuart Clark of CHS, is a dual board-certified physi-cian, one certified both as a family practitioner and in occupational health.

But it's certainly not the only approach. Midlevel nurse practi-tioners are common. Nurse practitioners are medical practitioners whose skills rank between those of a registered nurse and a physi-cian. Besides clinical care, they focus on health promotion, disease prevention, health education, and counseling; they emphasize "both care and cure," according to the American Society of Nurse Practi-tioners.

NPs are licensed in all states and the District of Columbia and they practice under the rules and regulations of the state in which they are licensed. "We are huge fans of [nurse] practitioners. They are highly functional," Clark says.

Patricia Berger-Friedman of Watson Wyatt also praises nurse prac-titioners because the connection with patients is so much greater: "They are better able to get people on track. There are no excuses. They're right there. They'll call you if you don't show up for an ap-pointment. They know who needs to be there for what."

Companies usually aren't in the business of practicing medicine, so although you could directly hire your own health-care professionals to staff the facility, you would do better to outsource. You can hire a third-party vendor to provide and manage the staff and services, or you can contract directly with outside health-care professionals to manage the facility.

When making that decision, make the effort to determine whether the provider has a real commitment to health promotion and will be an effective model for the company's wellness program. "An overweight physician who smokes will not be effective at promoting wellness," Gary Pritts says.

Questions to ask include: Does the provider have the tools for population health management and rigorous outcomes management? Are these integrated with an electronic medical record system? Does the provider have any conflicts of interest? For example, do they also own and operate the local hospital where they will benefit from referrals?

Harrah's corporate health and wellness centers, operated by Whole Health Management, provide a wide range of services, from vaccinations and treatment of infections and minor injuries to health education, nutrition counseling, and physical therapy. Clinical staff members diagnose and treat chronic conditions, such as diabetes and high blood pressure, and provide prescription medication.

Services at the Las Vegas medical clinic are available six days a week for any employee who participates in Harrah's health insurance plan, as well as for company-insured spouses and dependents as young as two. "Pretty much anything you can do at the doctor's office" is available at the health center, says Jacqueline Peterson. "Whole Health can take care of the whole person."

MODERN MODEL

Making on-site health services available—especially for treating minor illnesses and injuries and providing follow-up care—can reduce the number of visits employees make to more expensive facilities, such as hospital emergency rooms. An on-site facility helps your employees maintain better overall health and manage chronic health conditions, while it reduces the amount of time they spend away from work visiting off-site providers.

This modern model of on-site centers is proving to be cost-effective. "Not only does it pick up health issues earlier, but it doesn't require time away from work and at the same time creates a culture of caring," says Sean Sullivan, president, CEO and cofounder of the Institute for Health and Productivity Management, a nonprofit corporation in Scottsdale, Arizona.[10]

Toyota Motor Manufacturing Texas Inc. operates a multimillion-dollar health-care center next to its San Antonio vehicle assembly plant that is open to its employees, on-site suppliers, and families of both. The clinic offers primary, dental, and eye care as well as physical therapy. It also includes a lab and pharmacy.[11] It charges $5 per office visit and offers free generic drugs. There aren't many routine procedures the 20,000-square-foot clinic can't handle, says Dr. Stephen Carter, medical director for Take Care Health Systems, which manages the clinic. Trained staff do everything from basic blood work to ultrasound.

To meet the company's goal of making visits as quick and convenient as possible, the clinic is on a shared computer system. That means a radiologist can e-mail X-rays directly to a staff physician, and staff physicians can transfer prescriptions directly to the pharmacy—both of which cut patient wait times.[12] Employees can visit other doctors for a $15 to $30 copay, but the company reports that roughly two-thirds regularly choose the Toyota clinic.

American Cast Iron Pipe Co. in Birmingham, Alabama, has a 36,000-square-foot clinic to provide medical coverage for 8,800 employees, retirees, and dependents. The clinic has six full- and part-time doctors on staff, including two pediatricians, four pharmacists, five dentists, and 12 nurses, to handle 200 medical visits and 70 dental visits a day. Employees don't pay anything out of pocket for health insurance, but they do pay $10 for a doctor visit and 25 percent of the cost of prescriptions. If they choose to go to doctors outside of the clinic, they then pay a percentage of the cost.

Employees who are injured—either on the job or outside of work—can receive physical therapy at the on-site clinic and at the gym. After the American Cast Iron Pipe Co. brought its physical therapy services in-house in 2000, Rebecca Kelly, the company's wellness coordinator, says it was able to cut costs in half even while doubling the number of participants.[13]

A well-run clinic should provide all levels of care—primary, secondary, and tertiary care, says Fabius. "If they don't, they really aren't engaging in population health management."

Population health management is where health care and wellness meet. Population health management integrates and coordinates the delivery of all care that affects the health and productivity of an organization. That includes corporate wellness, disease management, catastrophic case management, utilization management, Employee Assistance Programs, disability, and/or worker's compensation programs.

"The old war cry was 'we're going to look for employees who have the skill and the will,' the training and the motivation to do the job well. I've been trying to propose to the leadership of the human resource world that it should be 'skill, will and not be ill.' That third component can offer a rethinking of the way employers invest in health," Fabius, of Walgreen's Health and Wellness division, says. "So many look at simply trying to reduce health-care cost, as opposed to take investment and use that money as wisely as possible to advance the productivity of the workforce."

THE BOTTOM LINE

No one argues that having an on-site fitness center or medical facility is cheap. But such facilities certainly make your employees' lives more convenient—and healthier. Your company can reap benefits as well. An on-site fitness center makes it easy for employees to get more exercise and to become and stay healthy. It can offer personalized instruction and even increase interaction among employees from various departments of your organization. An on-site health center promotes early medical intervention and treatment, which reduces the need for costly specialty care, emergency room usage, hospitalization and absence from work.

Your employees' physical health shouldn't be your only concern. Their mental health is just as crucial, and mental illness can certainly be as costly as physical illness. Chapter 8 deals with mental health concerns.

Profile: Taking It All On-Site (http://www.rbha.org)

Richmond Behavioral Health Authority (RBHA) has its own fitness center with a personal trainer and has a nurse on-site who oversees the employee health program. What it doesn't have is a lot of employees. In fact, its roughly 400-member workforce persuasively counters the argument that only large corporations can afford and maintain on-site facilities and personnel. RBHA's relatively young workforce—40 percent are under forty—have stressful jobs counseling Richmond, Virginia, residents who have mental health and substance abuse problems. "Some of the [clients'] stories are heartbreaking," says Charles D. Story, director of human resources, and so employees develop "an emotional attachment to the job" that can wear them down. To keep its workers healthy, RBHA has developed a wellness structure that includes stress management sessions as well as nutrition classes, a weight-loss program, and walking teams.

Employees who work out at the agency's fitness center get an hour and a half for lunch, rather than the usual hour. Despite the reduced work day, Story claims there's greater productivity for RBHA. "It's difficult to get a quantitative number as far as productivity gains, but you can see it in quality of work that is done. It's palpable." Offering these wellness services on-site "demonstrates our investment in employees, and it has retention values."

Another big plus is that health insurance premiums are falling. "While everyone else is getting increases, we've had a 12 percent decrease," he says, continuing a three-year trend of holding down health expenses.

RBHA shows that having an on-site fitness center doesn't have to be expensive, that there are ways to do it without spending tens of thousands of dollars. In 2004, RBHA turned part of a multipurpose room into a gym with an initial investment of $22,000 for commercial-quality equipment that was built to last.

Before opening the center, RBHA had offered a membership discount to outside gyms, and not one single person used it, according to Story's predecessor. He found it ineffectual for the HR department to try to coordinate outside gym memberships because the return on investment just wasn't there.

RBHA's gym is free, open 24 hours a day, and now has a full-time personal trainer who works a variable schedule. The gym has elliptical machines, treadmills, free weights, and body-building stations. Group exercise classes also are available.

What drives the program is its accessibility during normal office hours. "You don't have to take away from work or family. Everybody leads busy lives with a hundred reasons not to do exercise. This removes many of the barriers," Story says.

Family members of employees are encouraged to participate in the programs because there is significant evidence to support the theory that behavior modifications are most likely to stick of family members and friends also are committed to making similar changes.

Yet another benefit is that "you're bonding with people in different divisions, different areas of work that otherwise you would have no reason to encounter," Story says. That includes RBHA's CEO Wilson Washington.

RBHA addresses liability issues as if it were operating a health club, with employees signing a waiver that holds RBHA harmless.

A NURSE ON THE TEAM

In 2008, RBHA hired Megan Wellford, a registered nurse, to be the full-time wellness coordinator. She doesn't have a shiny, expensive equipment-filled clinic; she works out of the HR department.

Being part of the HR team "is a great place for me," she says, because it gives her quick access to information when she has questions about policies and procedures. "It's crucial to doing the job. I would advise making the position of wellness coordinator part of HR department to avoid obstacles that are likely to stand in the way," says Wellford.

It also makes it easy for employees to find her. "The benefits coordinator is just a stone's throw away. People stop by and say 'I was just curious about my blood pressure.' People stop me in the halls and the elevators," she says.

Employees not only feel safe visiting Wellford, she says, they find it convenient because it can save them trips to the doctor. Wellford does a lot of routine screenings such as blood pressure, blood glucose, cholesterol, and body mass index. But Wellford makes no pretense that she's a physician: "I don't venture out on medications. I may say, 'your blood pressure is a little on the high side, what are you doing?' I make referrals, I educate."

Her services are valuable to the company as well as to employees because Wellford can conduct preemployment screenings and administer tuberculin skin tests. "Because of our population, it's pretty high risk. That's a huge savings for the company," she says.

Plus, she recently became certified to teach CPR and lead group exercise classes for employees. RBHA also is paying for her to become certified as a personal fitness trainer so she can fill in for the regular trainer.

But it's the credentials she brought with her that Wellford believes makes the big difference. "I'm excited that RBHA went the extra mile and hired an RN," she says. "It allows me to make my nursing knowledge and skills available to people in an environment that is safe, convenient and familiar."

Chapter Eight

Mental Wellness Matters Too

The cost of mental illness is indisputably high. Mood disorders cause more work loss and impairment than common physical illnesses such as diabetes, asthma, and arthritis—an estimated $50 billion a year in lost productivity and nearly 321.2 million in lost workdays.[1]

Employees bring a host of serious problems with them to the job: major depression, bipolar disorder, chronic mild depression known as dysthymia, and substance abuse. Added to that are family and financial worries. Then the workplace adds its own pressures with information overload and productivity demands.

The effort to balance work and home responsibilities can take its toll, often in the form of stress. While there is no one definition of stress that everyone accepts, its physical, psychological, and emotional effects on employees are evident—as are its effects on job performance and efficiency.

More than half of men and women surveyed by the American Psychological Association—55 percent—said that stress reduced their productivity at work.[2] A later APA study found that nearly 80 percent of Americans surveyed said they were stressed about the economy and about their personal finances. About 47 percent reported having headaches, while 35 percent said they had upset stomachs, and 34 percent said they experienced muscular tension due to stress. Sixty percent of the poll respondents reported they were feeling angry and irritable, and 53 percent reported feeling fatigued. Forty-eight of those surveyed said that to cope with stress they had overeaten or eaten unhealthy food. Almost one-fifth of Americans reported drinking alcohol in an attempt to manage their stress (18 percent), and 16 percent reported smoking.[3]

THE MENTAL AFFECTS THE PHYSICAL

Mental health affects physical health in a number of ways, according to research by the American Psychological Association:

- More than 9 out of 10 (93%) of Americans surveyed said that perceptions, thoughts, and choices affect physical health (APA poll, 2005).

- More than half (58%) of Americans said they believe that one can't have good physical health without good mental health (APA poll, 2005).

- And more than one-third of Americans said they have had an illness that was primarily caused by stress (APA poll, 2005).

Health problems such as obesity, sleeping disorders, alcoholism, and tobacco use often have mental as well as physical components. Physical and mental health are so obviously interconnected that they can't, and shouldn't, be separated, making it imperative that you include mental health in your overall wellness efforts.

TREATMENT, PREVENTION SAVES MONEY

The good news is that the cost of prevention and treatment is less than many people believe and the benefit—for affected individuals and for the organizations that employee them—is great. For example, efforts to identify and treat depression in the workplace significantly improve employee health and productivity and are likely to lead to lower costs overall for the employer, notes a *Journal of the American Medical* Association report.[4]

The question, for individuals and organizations, is where to start. The most basic way to help employees deal with a range of mental-health issues is through an Employee Assistance Program. The EAP, usually administered by a third-party vendor, helps employees identify and resolve personal problems relating to health, family, finances, addiction, and stress. Increasingly, the EAP is the employer's—and employee's—entree into the mental health system. Sixty-five percent of employers provided EAPs in 2008, up from 56 percent 10 years before.[5]

The number of EAPs is growing because companies find their services effective. When EAP services are provided, work time loss can be avoided in 60 percent of cases with an average savings of 17 hours per case, according to a Family and Work Institute study. And 72 percent of the cases studied showed improved productivity with an average gain of 43 percent.[6] An EAP "is a core benefit . . . a very inexpensive benefit" that saves money by reducing other health-related costs, says Marina London, a spokesperson for the Employee Assistance Professionals Association (EAPA).

A good EAP vendor provides employees with confidential and timely problem identification, assessment, and counseling services. The vendor is in a position to refer employees to other health-care professionals for diagnosis, treatment, and assistance. The EAP vendor you choose should work hand in hand with your company's wellness committee because it's the members of the wellness committee who are in the best position to steer people who need EAP services to the program.

The EAP vendor and wellness committee also should be working together to promote services. Many companies buy an EAP service and leave all promotion up to the vendor, London says, but the vendor needs internal assistance to effectively reach employees. The program requires continual promotion because of employee turnover and because people tend not to pay attention to what services are offered until they need them.

When looking for an EAP vendor, London recommends "be honest with yourself in terms of what your budget is and what that budge is going to get you. Often organizations are looking just at the price. As with most things you get what you pay for." Taking the least expensive approach usually means restricting coverage for family members and limiting the number of sessions. Ideally, "you want a generous program that covers everybody in the household and is staffed by experienced people. You want 24 hour coverage, seven days a week," says London.

Too many companies buy the cheapest model and don't do their homework. "I'm amazed how un-businesslike business is" when it comes to choosing EAP services, says Dale Masi, president and CEO of Masi Research Consultants in Boston. A lot of EAPs try to deliver at a low price by not providing adequate services. "There should be educational programs once a month. There should be at health fairs and tip sheets for employees," says Masi. "Too often the EAP doesn't do follow up by getting [the employee] into an ongoing support system."

Liability is a particular concern if you are purchasing legal and financial services from EAPs. The Employee Assistance Professionals Association offers a buyers' guide to help companies identify suitable vendors and accreditation is available through the Council on Accreditation (http://www.coanet.org), which provides standards for private social service and behavioral health-care organizations.

Treat an EAP like any other product you would buy. Demand quality assurance and monitor services. Masi's company conducts telephone audits to check on vendors. "We act like clients. We find out, is somebody there in the middle of the night? I have callers call at midnight on Thanksgiving," she says.

FOCUS ON PREVENTION

Obviously, a good EAP can help your employees during times of crisis. But don't limit its scope; don't think of it in isolation as just another benefit. Increasingly EAPs are focusing on prevention as well as treatment. Make sure your EAP is working in concert with other types of benefits and wellness programs. Bring all of these components together to keep people physically and mentally healthy.

Some organizations promote mental health by taking more positive steps to prevent stress in the workplace and in employees' lives in general. Alternative benefits can go a long way toward alleviating workplace stress, say a pair of business law professors from the University of Michigan who studied *Fortune* magazine's list of the best companies to work for. The professors reported that the organizations on the list had significantly lower turnover that resulted in an average cost savings as a group of about $275 million in 2007.

The professors presented a typical list of benefits that can help relieve workplace stress: employer-paid health-care premiums, paid leave, telecommuting, flextime, subsidized health-care classes, health club memberships, and on-site medical clinics and fitness centers.

More unusual items on the list included valet parking, laundry and dry-cleaning services, grocery delivery, and special services for employees who are new parents. The list also included discounted tickets to outside-of-work social activities such as plays, museums, movies, sporting events, and amusement parks.[7]

The American Psychological Association honors organizations that promote employee health and well-being while enhancing organizational performance and productivity. Its Psychologically Healthy Workplace Award (PHWA) is based on five categories: health and safety, work-life balance, employee involvement, employee growth and development, and employee recognition.

The award doesn't recognize an organization just for taking a feel-good approach to mental wellness; it emphasizes the return on investment that results from a psychologically healthy workplace. For example, the APA cites 2008 winner Teledyne Brown Engineering, which had a 34 percent reduction in absenteeism due to its wellness program. The company found that employees who participated in the program used one-third fewer sick days than those who did not participate.

The five 2008 PHWA winners reported an overall average turnover rate of 11 percent in 2008, less than the national average of 39 percent reported by the Bureau of Labor Statistics.[8] Additionally, 87 percent of employees in the APA survey said they would recommend their organizations to others as a good place to work, compared to 44 percent overall. And only 5 percent said they intended to look for employment elsewhere within the next year, compared to 32 percent overall.

The winning organizations found that only a quarter of employees reported experiencing chronic work stress, compared to 39 percent nationally, according to the APA survey, and 85 percent of employees reported that they were satisfied with their jobs, compared to only 61 percent overall.[9]

Creating a psychologically healthy workplace means much more than fixing problems, says Dr. David W. Ballard, APA assistant executive director of corporate relations and business strategy. "It's about promoting good health, enhancing performance and creating a work environment where both employees and the organization can thrive."

Flexible work arrangements, programs promoting healthy lifestyle behavior and choices, employee participation in the decision-making process, leadership development, and skills training are some of the qualities that help define a psychologically healthy workplace. Many executives still see such initiatives as a cost, not a benefit, to the company, but Ballard finds "there's been a great deal of work done trying to look at the links between highly engaged and excited employees and the benefits that accrue to the corporation or organization—benefits that include innovation, collaboration, greater customer satisfaction, reduced costs in many cases and . . . greater productivity and profitability at the bottom line."

Any type of organization, large or small, has the power and the responsibility to create a psychologically healthy workplace, Ballard believes. If you want your organization to be more psychologically healthy, first look at all of your wellness initiatives and decide how best to incorporate mental wellness. Don't just treat problems as they arise. That's the most expensive approach. It's more effective to prevent as many problems as possible from coming up in the first place by creating and maintaining a flexible, supportive environment.

Good communications is critical, and, as in other areas of wellness, senior managers must walk the talk. But also make sure you get plenty of employee input because if the employees don't help shape the program, it won't meet the real needs of your workforce.

While there is no denying that an economic downturn may require some belt-tightening, "employers should be careful not to secure this quarter's financial returns at the expense of employee well-being or the organization's long-term success," Ballard says. He recommends tying a psychologically healthy workplace to the mission and values and goals of the organization because "especially in tough economic times, programs that aren't tied in to the mission and goals are easy to cut."

FLEXIBILITY AND FUN

Each year, the American Psychological Association recognizes organizations for the ways they encourage employee involvement, better health and safety, employee growth and development, work-life balance, and employee recognition. The various winners of APA's Psychologically Healthy Workplace Award provide a mix of tried-and-true benefits and unusual ones, all designed to reduce stress and increase productivity.

Porter Keadle Moore, LLP (http:www.pkm.com)

The Atlanta-based accounting and consulting firm prides itself in helping its employees to balance their work-life obligations, utilizing tailored solutions such as flexible scheduling, part-time employment, and work-from-home options. The firm encourages such flexibility because it values the results that employees produce rather than just the number of hours they work, says Debbie Sessions, partner and chief operating officer. "We can do our work any time, any place, as long as we meet our clients' needs."

Of the nearly 100 people working at Porter Keadle Moore, about 15 percent have formalized their flexible work arrangements. But in reality, Sessions says, "I believe 100 percent of us work flexible hours. We've been doing this for over 20 years."

Allowing greater flexibility has been especially helpful in retaining talented women with children. It says to these women that "we'd rather have you some of the time than none. We get what we need and you get what you need," Sessions says, adding that the flexibility motivates other employees too because they realize how much the firm is willing to do for individuals.

And while many firms say they are "family friendly," at some firms, some executives don't act it, she says. "Ours live it. They coach their kids' teams. Our people see that." Sessions says the firm recognizes that "the whole person comes to work."

The firm closes its office during the last week in December to help employees prepare for the stress of its busy January to April tax season. It closes two hours early on Fridays during the summer.

Health benefits at Porter Keadle Moore, including mental health coverage, Employee Assistance Program services, and wellness programs, take effect on the day an employee begins work. The firm encourages leadership growth and development through coaching and the use of a corporate psychologist. "That's part of the recruiting process for our management team. He does testing to help us understand the individuals who will manage the organizations," according to Sessions.

Porter Keadle Moore partners with other accounting firms to provide employee training and engages employees in games to hone conflict-resolution and problem-solving skills. The firm developed a career-track guide that outlines the personal leadership and technical expectations of all employees. It offers incentives for employees who are seeking certifications and other professional designations, with paid time off to study and monetary bonuses for passing exams.

The firm regularly conducts surveys to get feedback about such things as leadership, culture, rewards, and work content. It even applies its employee involvement principles to its group insurance renewal process. Employees served on a task force where they learned about vendor and benefits selection as well as how the appropriate use of benefits can help both individuals and the organization.

Porter Keadle Moore encourages both physical and mental well-being. It supports a range of physical activities through corporate-sponsored basketball, flag football, and tennis teams. Weekly competitions and games provide rewards and recognition, and the firm organizes social activities, such as after-work social gatherings, sporting events, and spa retreats. There's even a weekly delivery to the office of organic fruit.

Healthwise (http://www.healthwise.org)

As a publisher, Healthwise gives consumers information to help them make better health decisions. As an employer, the Boise, Idaho–based nonprofit organization helps its employees achieve better physical and mental health.

The organization's efforts have paid off. Its turnover rate of 8 percent is nearly 20 percent lower than the industry average, and the company receives 125 to 150 applications for every job opening. Annual revenue climbed to from $15.9 million in 2004 to $22.5 million in 2007, the year the *Wall Street Journal* rated it one of the nation's Top Small Workplaces.[10]

Healthwise's approximately 200 employees consistently rank workplace flexibility as one of the organization's most attractive features. Additional work-life efforts include family-friendly policies, an extra holiday for each employee on his or her birthday, and a dogs-at-work program.

"We try to recognize that folks spend a full one third of their lives at work. They will be happier if there are fewer barriers" between work and other aspects of their lives, says Molly Mettler, Healthwise senior vice president of mission. "Family members are welcome at any time in our workplace."

Healthwise wellness coordinator Jan Nissl says that as a single parent she takes advantage of her company's family-oriented flexibility. Many other employees do so too, she says, noting that one vice president spent one week a month in northern Idaho, working remotely, to take care of her elderly parents.

Healthwise makes it easy for employees to exercise, with a fitness room, on-site exercise and yoga classes, locker rooms with showers, and company bikes. It is close to hiking and biking trails. The company also makes it easy to relax. There are two quiet rooms for naps or nursing, a sun deck, an outdoor dining area, and a hammock.

Its wellness program includes an Employee Assistance Program and up to $250 per year per employee in Wellness Bucks for making healthy lifestyle and behavior choices. The annual Healthwise Wellness Day features fitness assessments, health screenings, guest speakers, and personal goal setting. Throughout the year, lunch-and-learn sessions cover topics ranging from nutrition to acupuncture to CPR. Employees receive copies of Healthwise's own handbook that covers 200 common health issues, and they have free access to the online Healthwise Knowledgebase.

The employee-centered approach to training and development features "Healthwise Way," a comprehensive program designed to enhance learning and professional growth. The company provides financial assistance for continuing education and sponsors a volunteer "Mentor Corps" to help new employees make a smooth transition into the organization.

Staff members gather in the lobby each week for a healthy snack and a short break to connect with coworkers. Each month, staff meetings are the forum for recognition award presentations for service excellence and innovation. The organization hosts "Inside Healthwise," an orientation for families and partners of each new employee, as well as an annual picnic and holiday party for employees and their families. "We have a Halloween party where kids come in for [noncandy] treats and people can take home ideas about healthy snacks. That's a more subtle way of including the family" in making wise wellness choices, Nissl says.

The company also partners with charitable organizations and encourages volunteering in the community. "That plays a role in overall wellness. It gives some stress release because it feel good giving back," she says.

Green Mountain Coffee Roasters (http://www. greenmountaincoffee.com)

The Waterbury, Vermont–based company goes a long way to encourage employees to keep mentally and physically fit. It also sends employees a long way, to better immerse them in the company's mission of creating long-term solutions and sustainability for people and ecosystems worldwide.

The company sends groups of employees on what it calls *origins trips*—visits to the farms and co-ops in Latin America where tons of coffee beans are hand picked and processed. Green Mountain prides itself in guaranteeing farmers a minimum price that's often higher than the market rate and also ensures that producers meet social and environmental standards.

So far, about 20 percent of the company's 1,250 employees have made trips, which are designed to give them an appreciation of the role they and the company play in improving the lives of poor farmers, says Betsy Stanford, HR specialist. "They can see how poor the communities may be if a company is buying at sub-standard levels. They can see the difference we're making. Employees understand that we're the ones paying fair trade and going organic. They can see that what they do every day makes a difference," Stanford says. "If employees have a better understanding of the care and difference we can make in buying from these places, it adds a whole other level of connection" to the company.

At home, Green Mountain Coffee Roasters has won praise for its attention to both physical and mental health, commitment to flexible work arrangements, and training and development opportunities. The company promotes a sense of social responsibility with its program that allows employees to donate an hour per week to non-profit work.

The company says, in return for its efforts, it gets better financial performance, increased productivity, and a reduced rate of workplace injury and illness. Work-life balance and opportunities for education and advancement are key to keeping turnover low. The goal is to develop employees and have them grow with the company, Stanford says. "We care about the development and morale of employees. We want to keep them, [and] keep them happy. We have people here who have a history with us."

The company pays for educational programs, including personal development classes. The goal is to have at least 30 hours or training, per employee per year. Stanford cites herself as an example of the success of the educational program. She was an executive secretary before receiving the training to run the HR department.

Green Mountain Coffee Roasters is mindful of employees' physical safety and health. Each worker receives a $500 annual allowance to use for fitness-related activities such as joining a health club or taking swimming lessons. Employees can receive a discount on insurance premiums by participating in designated wellness initiatives

MENTAL PARITY

Does the Mental Health Parity and Addiction Equity Act affect your organization? Two questions: Do you provide medical and surgical benefits? Do you have more than 50 employees?

If you answer yes to both, then, as of 2010, you will have to make sure that your mental health benefits are on par with your physical illness coverage. Group health plans that provide both medical/surgical benefits and mental health/substance-use disorder benefits will not be able to impose financial requirements and limitations to those mental health benefits that are more restrictive than restrictions to the other benefits. That includes copayments and deductibles, and limitations such as number of visits or frequency of treatments.

If your organization does not provide medical and surgical benefits, or has fewer than 50 employees, the act does not apply.

Groups that had opposed the act warned that mental parity would increase health-care costs, but states that already have such mental health parity laws haven't seen increases.[11]

such as taking a health assessment or joining a walking, running, or biking program.

Employees and their family members have access to an EAP and meditation, facilitated by two instructors, is available on site. "If you're mind is so concerned with something in your personal life, you won't be doing an excellent job," Stanford says. "We're trying to support employees in every part of their lives that we can. Happy people are better workers."

THE BOTTOM LINE

More organizations are getting the message that mental health matters as much as physical health. If you want to join that group, start with an Employee Assistance Program (EAP). Usually run by a third-party vendor, an EAP can help your employees identify and resolve personal problems relating to health, family, finances, addiction, and stress. A good EAP vendor will provide your employees with confidential and timely problem identification, assessment, and counseling services and can refer employees to other health-care professionals for diagnosis, treatment, and assistance.

In addition to providing an EAP, look for ways your organization can be more like those Psychologically Healthy Workplace Award winners that have found creative solutions to reducing employee's stress and increasing their productivity.

Next, chapter 9 looks at resources in your community that can help you keep employees healthy.

Profile: A Garden with Mentally Healthy Delights (http://www.apa.org)

A *green* roof, complete with a garden and a labyrinth, is the most visible sign of the American Psychological Association's commitment to having a wholly healthy workforce. It's part of the association's efforts to promote the physical, mental, and emotional well being of its employees and the well being of the environment too.

The roof-garden, atop one of the Washington, D.C.–based association's two buildings, helps the environment by reducing the "urban heat island effect," at the same time acting as insulation to reduce energy consumption.

The greenery helps with water and air purification as well as giving visitors a place for quiet reflection. The labyrinth, a circular walking path, provides a contemplative space for meditation and introspection. Unlike a maze, a labyrinth has no false paths—one path leads to the center and out again.

With its Psychologically Healthy Workplace Award, the APA recognizes other exceptional organizations that effectively foster total employee health and well-being while enhancing performance and productivity. The association is dedicated to achieving, for its own employees, the goals it has set for award winners: work-life balance; health and safety; and employee involvement, growth, development, and recognition.

"We went through our own evaluation process. We thought if we're giving these awards we should hold ourselves to the same standard," says Dr. David W. Ballard, assistant executive director of corporate relations and business strategy. "We try to practice what we preach."

RICH MENTAL HEALTH PLAN

The association has many traditional wellness initiatives in place: flexible work arrangements, fitness opportunities, and healthy food choices. But the initiative that Human Resources Director Ismael Rivera is particularly proud of is the APA's rich mental health outpatient plan that covers dependents as well as employees. "It's rare because, Number 1, we pay for it. And, we offer it to employees even if they don't enroll in our plan," he says.

Rivera's also proud of the association's Employee Assistance Program, which is managed by an independent third party to protect employee confidentiality. Working with general information he receives from the vendor about usage, Rivera looks at categories such as job stress, family issues, and addiction, "so we have a sense of possible trends" that require attention.

The EAP's skills have been put to the test. "One time we had a situation where a well- regarded coworker passed away unexpectedly," Rivera says, and EAP staff members stepped in to counsel employees.

Each month APA invites EAP representatives to take part in the association's orientation program so that new employees "can hear directly from them about what the services are and what they do. And new employees will know at least one person [at the EAP] by name," Rivera says.

The association's wellness initiative includes lunch-and-learns, health fair screenings, and nutritional counseling. APA prides itself in good safety practices and offers a free ergonomic assessment program.

Programs are tailored to make sure way they meet the specific needs of employees and are tied into the mission, values, and goals of the organization. When the association opened the newer of its two buildings in 1992, it opened up a lot of opportunities for new policies and programs, says Holly Siprelle, director of staff initiatives. "We got a committee together to enhance our benefits. It was an eye opener. One of our turning points was getting Bright Horizons"—child care facilities—on-site.

Both APA buildings have fitness centers that are open 24 hours a day. The centers don't have trainers on-site, but employees can arrange for access to a personal trainer. The fitness center has proved to be an incentive that attracts other tenants in APA's buildings. It helps with employee retention too, Siprelle says. "People tell us in their exit interviews that it is one of the things they will miss."

Not all the programs require much space. Siprelle says she's organized yoga and meditation in her own office. Space also is made available for Weight Watchers classes and subsidized upper- body massage. The building has bike racks for people who pedal to work.

One of the side benefits of the APA's rich portfolio of physical and mental wellness initiatives is that "it gets people out of their silos. Our goal is that we want to get people to connect in new and fresh ways . . . It's another way of introducing us to each other as human beings and as a community," she believes.

Chapter Nine

Working Together: Partners in Prevention

They're patients, they're health-care consumers, they're your employees. How can your organization partner with the medical community to keep the people who work for you as healthy and productive as possible?

When you know where to look, you can find hospitals, insurers, local wellness councils, and boards of health that are eager to step up to help you stretch your finite resources. Local hospitals can be great sources of education programs, screenings, and health assessments. They're not being altruistic. There's something in it for them—more business. This type of outreach "repositions the hospital as a provider of solutions to the issue of employee health costs, rather than just another contributor to the problem. The hospitals hope to link at-risk employees to the health-care services they need while creating loyalty between the hospital and its physicians. In essence, health-management collaboration is customer relationship management at its most personal level," according to Aegis Health Group Inc.[1]

Hospitals usually rely on health insurers or brokers or agents to be their face to the public. "They aren't always positioning themselves in the best light. We try to get hospitals to get out in the sunshine and be a leader. If you stay in the shadows, you set yourself up to be the villain," says Henry E. Ross, president and ECO of Aegis, based in Brentwood, Tennessee. Aegis works with acute-care hospitals that want to create relationships with commercially insured employers, particularly midsize employers.

Companies tend to find it odd, but refreshing, that local hospitals are willing to talk to them frankly about health-care costs and are willing to tell them that what the companies have been doing doesn't work anymore. They "can raise the deductible and co-pays and push a little more to employees but there's not much more meat on that bone," Ross says. It's time, with the hospital's aid, to focus on prevention.

Where exactly do you start? Look for a hospital's business development/marketing department, not the business office, which does billing. These are the people who are responsible for bringing patients/customers through their doors. That means they need your employees.

Hospitals may seem to be intimidating and to have a complicated business model, but they're really pretty straightforward, says Bradley Mabry, director of business development for Ennis Regional Medical Center in Ennis, Texas. "Hospitals want that business. If you talk to the right person the hospital will want to do the lion's share" of the work to win your employees as customers.

Mabry is the person to talk to at Ennis Regional Medical Center. "I find out what your insurance companies are, I prepare lunch and invite the company's CEO or the director of HR to talk about what we can do for them." Why? Because if one of your employees comes to the hospital for health education or screenings, that employee will become familiar with the hospital and be more likely to return, when necessary. "If you kid breaks a leg and if you have choice to make, you'll say 'I'm going to Ennis Regional.' We've made the relationship stronger," says Mabry.

SUITE OF TOOLS

One of Aegis' goals is to make sure that employers and hospitals are on the same page. "We bring in a suite of tools, mainly software modeling tools, to help employers understand where their health risks are" and what actions need to be taken, Ross says.

The first step toward a healthier workforce is a health assessment to get a baseline measurement (see chapter 6). Employee privacy is protected, Ross emphasizes. The personal health information belongs to the hospital, not the insurance company and the hospital "has to treat it like any other medical record." Generally, the hospital is paying to gather the information from the assessment and can make the aggregate data available to employers at no cost. Once the information has been gathered and aggregated, the hospital can work with the employer to set priorities. "You don't want to be over-whelming. You can say 'Here are the top three risks—which do you want to take first?'" he says.

The hospital can work with the employer to concentrate on prevention, dealing with the lowest cost alternatives first. Typically, it starts with education in four main areas of modifiable behaviors: tobacco use, diet and nutrition, fitness and exercise, and stress and depression.

The hospital is seen by members of the community as a trusted local hub that is in a position to coordinate physicians and other health providers, such as nutritionists. The hospital "can bring in the right people to take the solution to the workplace and make it easy for companies to make the first step," Ross says. Obviously physicians have an important role to play in wellness, he adds, but the economics of the current health-care system do not reward doctors for keeping people healthy, only for doing for procedures and appointments.

INSURERS GETTING THE WORD

Health insurance companies are getting the word about the importance of preventive care services. They're getting the word from people like you.

Benefits departments in companies are moving beyond their traditional roles, says Patrick Leary, director of external relations at the National Committee for Quality Assurance. Some are going "straight to the provider to force the integration of medical, disability, health promotion, prevention, and productivity programs."[2]

Wellness was the most highly valued noncore service offered by health plans according to a PricewaterhouseCooper survey. About 80 percent of large employers surveyed ranked wellness services almost as high in importance as provider discounts and accurate claims processing.

Health insurers that want to improve their satisfaction ratings need to offer services that are most important to their clients and services that are seen as delivering value, notes the PricewaterhouseCoopers report: "[S]ervices that rank high in importance but lower in satisfaction—such as provider discounts and wellness programs—deserve immediate attention." Employers that are looking

for effective wellness programs increasingly recognize the importance of incentives. So insurers can particularly distinguish themselves by integrating the most relevant incentives for an employee
group into benefit specifications, according to the report. Health
insurers have plenty of opportunity for innovation in this area.[3]

INNOVATIVE HEALTH INSURER INITIATIVES: PRIMEFITNESS

PrimeWest Health's PrimeFitness program uses health promotion, fitness facilities, clinics, hospitals, and professionals
in the community to increase physical activity, exercise, and
healthy living.

PrimeFitness takes the reimbursement system used by
most health plans for clinicians and applies it to health promotion and fitness professionals. PrimeWest Health con-
tracts with credentialed exercise specialists who work with
members to increase their amount of physical activity and
exercise.

PrimeWest Health members who choose to participate
receive an individualized fitness plan, created and implemented under the direction of fitness professionals. Participation in the program covers up to 28 visits with a fitness
professional over a one-year period, based on personal health
and fitness needs and specifically identified goals.

The health plan has targeted a wide variety of venues to
incorporate activity in the lives of members, including state
parks, hotel pools, physical therapy clinics, gyms, and nursing homes with exercise facilities. This unique health benefit
institutes a policy allowing PrimeFitness participants to use
those venues as a covered benefit.

To effectively identify members' needs and elicit positive
changes in health, PrimeFitness fitness professionals will
follow a specific protocol:

1. Collaborate with member's primary care physician
2. Administer health and fitness assessments

3. Assist with goal setting and the development of long-range health and fitness plans for individuals or groups

4. Provide personal training (individual or group fitness programs)

5. Provide regular consultations and evaluations

6. Record member's participation and progress and report to designated care providers

PrimeFitness goes beyond simply helping pay for a gym membership. It is aimed at promoting health and well-being and preventing disease by helping members make behavioral and environmental adaptations through education, guidance, and empowerment. The health plan envisions a collaborative network of PrimeWest members and families, fitness professionals, physicians, county health professionals and case managers, community education directors and instructors, and school district physical education and health education teachers, with all parties working together to promote physical activity and healthy lifestyles.

Adapted from *Innovations in Prevention, Wellness and Risk Reduction Innovations in Prevention, Wellness and Risk Reduction*, America's Health Insurance Plans, 2008.

Health insurers do "believe strongly that wellness programs are an important benefit option. Health plans have a wide variety of innovative programs, a variety of structures to meet individual needs of consumers or employers. They can help design a wellness program to meet [specific] needs," says Robert Zirkelbach, a spokesman for America's Health Insurance Plans (AHIP).

Most health plans provide, at the least, Web-based health and wellness information and support, and many are collaborating with employers to offer comprehensive programs at the worksite and beyond. A growing number have in-house health promotion departments, and some health plans have created free-standing companies that provide wellness services nationally.[4]

Health insurers not only help employers educate their workers, they educate physicians as well, Zirkelbach says. "Collaboration with physicians is important any time you do any wellness program because the physician is the one who is providing the care."

Health insurance companies that are not employing wellness are resisting the natural evolutionary pull of the industry, according to Dr. Dee W. Edington, director of the Health Management Research Center at the University of Michigan. "The model for the old-fashioned indemnity insurance company was the higher the health care costs, the more money it made," says Edington. "Then on the HMO side, if they can reduce costs they can make money because they're capitated," a payment system in which fees are paid per person and a provider is financially responsible for coordinating patient care within the fees rate. As insurance companies have moved to "health plans," that has made a difference, he says. "Insurance companies just pay for sickness. Health plans pay for sickness and wellness. Health plans are the drivers of this next generation of health care."[5]

The vast majority (more than 90% in most cases) of health insurers have plans that recommend and cover a core set of preventive care services, including vaccinations and screenings for cervical and colorectal cancer, according to a survey conducted by the American Association of Health Plans. Just short of 90 percent offer a free or low-cost smoking cessation program, and 81 percent recommend the use of smoking cessation aids to their enrollees who smoke, but only 48 percent covered the cost of smoking cessation devices and medications. HMOs, in particular have enhanced the use of preventive care, according to Health Plan Employer Data and Information Set (HEDIS).[6]

CONSUMER-DRIVEN PLANS

The trend toward consumer-driven health plans (CDHP) may be a bane, or a boon, for preventive care services. Forty-five percent of U.S. employers offered a consumer-driven plan in 2008 (like Health Savings Accounts), up from 37 percent the previous year, according to the International Society of Certified Employee Benefit Specialists (ISCEBS) and Aon Consulting.

Shifting costs and risk to consumers by making them responsible for the first $1,000 to $3,000 of their care before insurance kicks in (using in part dollars their employer gives them) could serve to either undermine or strengthen preventive health services. If, for example, consumers have to pay more out-of-pocket for preventive services, they are likely to use them less. But if employers structure consumer-driven plans so that preventive care benefits are covered free, or with very low copayments, enrollees may actually use the services more than they would in other kinds of plans.[7]

Health insurers can use well-designed consumer-driven plans to reinforce personal accountability as the core of wellness programs. Destiny Health, for example, rewards members with what it calls Vitality Bucks, which can be exchanged for merchandise for participating in fitness workouts, health screenings, and smoking cessation programs.

Humana has 421,000 members in its various consumer-driven plans, about 13 percent of its total membership. Members receive "HealthMiles" points for exercising; tracking blood pressure, weight, and body fat; and for reaching health and fitness goals. Members can redeem points at stores such as Target, Home Depot, or Best Buy.

According to a Humana study of 13,000 consumer-driven plan members in 155 companies, customers using these plans had annual claims-cost increases of between 5 percent and 6 percent, compared with double-digit increases in other plans.[8]

People in consumer-driven health plans are more cost-conscious than non-CDHP consumers, according to a 2008 Blue Cross/Blue Shield Association survey. The survey found that CDHP enrollees are more likely to track their health expenses than those in more traditional health insurance plans and are likely to question their physicians about treatment costs.

It also appears that people in consumer-driven plans are more likely to have regular physicals and preventive screenings than enrollees in traditional health plans and are more likely to participate in wellness-related activities programs, including exercise, health coaching, nutrition and diet counseling, stress management, and smoking cessation.[9]

ONE-ON-ONE COACHING

Health coaching is one way more and more health insurers are helping companies provide preventive-care services. Health coaches work with employees on a one-on-one basis primarily through phone calls, providing health reminders and information to help members become more knowledgeable about a wide variety of conditions. Coaches also encourage individuals to follow up regularly with their doctors.

INNOVATIVE HEALTH INSURER INITIATIVES:
REGENCE VITALITY PROGRAM

Regence's Vitality program helps employers build a culture of wellness through personalized support, care management programs, online tools, worksite wellness initiatives, and rewards.

A strong partnership between Regence and the employer is essential to Vitality's success. Personal wellness consultants work with each group to develop an overall wellness strategy. By assessing the organization's objectives, wellness goals, communication methods, and senior-level support, wellness consultants are able to guide the development of a customized wellness plan. As the employer puts the plan into action, Regence provides tools and continuous support to enable the employer to establish a solid infrastructure of health and wellness in the workplace. Regence wellness consultants also help employers administer surveys and assessment tools to collect baseline and follow-up data so employers can continue to customize and refine their wellness strategies.

Regence Vitality provides a wide variety of programs and resources to help employees take charge of their health: myRegence.com is a comprehensive source of information where members can access original health and lifestyle content, compare hospital cost and quality, research medications and cost-saving generics, search for a provider and review claims, explore care options with the medical library, and join community message boards.

Regence Health Coach provides personalized support by working one-on-one with members who have goals such as managing their weight, increasing physical activity, making healthy food choices, managing stress, and lowering cholesterol. In conjunction with RegenceRx, Regence Health Coach offers a unique sleep-improvement program to help members overcome sleep problems and find effective alternatives to sleep medication.

CareEnhance registered nurses are available 24/7 to answer health-related questions and help members make informed decisions about when, where (or if) to seek care.

Special Beginnings gives pregnant women deliver healthy babies their choice of a maternity book or DVD, materials tailored to their needs, and toll-free access to a nurse hotline 24/7.

Biometric screenings are available to provide employees with an assessment of basic health indicators, including blood pressure, body mass index (BMI), cholesterol, and glucose. Employees receive an analysis and explanation of their screening results and an aggregate de-identified report is delivered to the employer.

Regence provides a base incentive program available to all members, which rewards participants who engage in healthy behaviors with points they can exchange for gift cards.

Wellness consultants work with employers to plan health fairs and encourage maximum participation in a wide range of customized worksite initiatives, such as walking and healthy eating programs. They also provide continuing support to help educate employees about important health and wellness issues.

Adapted from *Innovations in Prevention, Wellness and Risk Reduction Innovations in Prevention, Wellness and Risk Reduction,* America's Health Insurance Plans, 2008.

For example, Blue Cross and Blue Shield of North Carolina, Chapel Hill, offers 11 separate types of health coaching programs focused on stress management, high blood pressure, high cholesterol, asthma, coronary artery disease, diabetes, migraine, fibromyalgia, prenatal care, tobacco cessation, and weight management.

Independence Blue Cross (IBC), Philadelphia offers health coaching for patients with any of 22 chronic and complex conditions. An IBC study found that the plan's disease management program lowered medical cost trends by nearly 3 percent during the program's second year and improved the health of members with chronic illnesses. More than 235,000 IBC members have at least one of the five most common chronic illnesses—diabetes, asthma, chronic obstructive pulmonary disease, congestive heart failure, and coronary artery disease—and 98 percent participate in the coaching program.

At Aetna, registered nurses in the plan's case and disease management program also have been trained in health coaching to answer questions, promote lifestyle changes, and encourage members to follow treatment plans. Disease management and case management staff generally work with 20 percent of the plan's membership who have chronic conditions, while wellness coaches "deal with portions of the other 80 percent of members, some of whom may have looming health risks," says Betsy Nota-Kirby, a wellness design leader at for the Hartford, Connecticut–based company.[10]

Yet another key contribution health insurers are making to workplace health promotion is helping employers link data on health conditions to medical costs. "Using this information, health plans can offer benefit designs that help employers make the appropriate investments in programs, and measure the impact of programs on medical costs," says Michael O'Donnell, editor in chief and president of the *American Journal of Health Promotion.* [11]

Staycee Benjamin is an employer consulting/worksite wellness program manager for Kaiser Permanente in Atlanta. In that role she works with HR representatives from large and midsize companies who are in charge of productivity and wellness initiatives. Benjamin helps companies host mini-health fairs, schedule massage therapists, and line up chefs to give seminars on healthy cooking, with Kaiser absorbing part of the cost of the programs.

Kaiser can offer an employer a template for a wellness initiative, but it prides itself on customizing a plan. "We get [companies] to look at their employees, to do surveys. We put all of that together and decide what works best. We try to get them to dig a little deeper. They may have workers in the field who have back pain or carpel tunnel," she says. Working with one company's claims data "we found that a lot of females had abnormal bleeding problems, so we did workshops on women's health issues."

Large companies that have multiple insurance carriers "find they like our services because they're a little different," Benjamin says. "Our whole campaign is about people making better choices about their lives. We want to really help make a change, to improve people's health. We want to change lives, not just have a great event."

Kaiser's electronic records system allows employees to receive newsletters, e-mail their doctors, look at lab results, schedule appointments, and share information. An employee isn't required to have information sent to his/her physician, but if the individual does opt to share, "it's a conduit between the doctor and patient. You can take your health risk assessment and send the results to your doctor," Benjamin says. And when a patient leaves the doctor the individual receives an after-visit summary of resources related to his/her specific health needs.

THE BROKER'S ROLE

You don't have to venture out into the insurance market alone. The right insurance broker can help you find the right health plan.

A conversation with a broker can set you on the path to a plan that best suits your needs, says Dario Campolattaro, a financial representative with Northwestern Mutual in Leesburg, Virginia. "Most insurance companies have invested in building pretty robust wellness systems, it's a matter of asking what's available."

In the past brokers have been too passive, says Beau Reid, vice president of employee benefits for Holmes Murphy & Associates, an independent risk management and insurance brokerage firm based in Des Moines, Iowa. As the cost of health has continued to go up, "it dawned on us that the way traditional brokers have done their job has not been effective. They go out every couple of years and hope costs get reduced. It doesn't work. We feel if companies aren't doing something, they won't be able get health insurance in five years."

Instead of simply saying "'can we bid your insurance,' we say 'where is the backdoor where money is leaking out of your business?' 'What do you think the root costs are?'" Reid says. He helps the company identify and reach out to the employees who are healthy but are at risk, the ones who are not chronically ill but are developing signs of chronic illness. The goal, he says, is to stop these employees from migrating into the chronically ill bucket.

Once programs are in place to reduce these expensive health risks, the company needs to establish metrics and measure results. The ability to create leverage in the marketplace is based upon credible data that is a combination of "biometric measures and corresponding reduction in risk that a company can demonstrate over time. Superimposed over that is the health-care cost per person. We like to take wellness data superimposed on health-care data and start charting some trends," he says.

INNOVATIVE HEALTH INSURER INITIATIVES:
HEALTHY BLUE LIVING

Blue Care Network's Healthy Blue Living program rewards members, employers, and physicians for working in concert to improve health behaviors. The program targets six modifiable health measures that are major drivers of poor health and high use of medications: alcohol use, smoking, blood pressure, cholesterol, blood sugar, and weight.

All members who sign up for the program receive higher benefits through reduced deductibles and copayments for the initial 90 days. In order to continue receiving this enhanced benefit level, participants must fill out an online health appraisal and schedule a visit with their primary care physician to complete a qualification form, which assesses the six modifiable health measures and includes biometric data such as blood pressure, cholesterol, body mass index, and blood sugar.

Participants must demonstrate to their physician that they are working to meet the goals of the action plans they developed in conjunction with their physicians and to maintain a healthy lifestyle. If they are a smoker, they must enroll in the Blue Care Network of Michigan's smoking cessation program "Quit the Nic." Members who do not complete the program requirements are moved to the standard benefits where they will have higher deductibles and copayments.

Healthy Blue Living helps members reach their goals through a variety of programs, including health coaching, smoking cessation, and weight management programs, as well as fitness center memberships, nutrition counseling, Web-based resources, newsletters, reminder cards, and specialized programs available to members who have been diagnosed with a chronic disease.

Employers offering Healthy Blue Living must commit to providing a healthy workplace and supporting their employees in reaching their goals. Blue Care Network performs an environmental assessment of the workplace, and all employers are required to provide a smoke-free work environment. Depending on the number of participating employees, employers must commit to offering health fairs, publishing health-related articles in employee publications, offering on-site classes, and providing healthy food choices in the cafeteria and vending machines.

Physicians receive a financial incentive for completing the members' qualification form, and they determine how often participants must follow up with them to discuss their progress. The minimum is once every two years, and smokers are required to actively participate in the smoking cessation program and follow up with their physician three months after enrollment. The forms were originally paper based, but now can be submitted electronically.

Adapted from *Innovations in Prevention, Wellness and Risk Reduction Innovations in Prevention, Wellness and Risk Reduction*, America's Health Insurance Plans, 2008.

When the company can show a positive trend in reducing risk and cost, particularly a multiple year trend, "we can take that to the insurance marketplace, and tell carriers we need our pricing to be discounted because of the risk management that we're applying," Reid says, expressing confidence that health insurers will want the business and will come up with their best offer. Holmes Murphy & Associates has its own wellness program, and its health-care costs have remained flat, says Reid, so "we know it works."

BOARDS AND COUNCILS

Local and state boards of health can be good sources of education, training, and technical assistance in your quest for employee wellness. Start with your local—usually county—board of health, and if it doesn't have a wellness coordinator who can help you promote healthy behavior at your organization, move up to the state level. You can find information through the National Association of Local Boards of Health (http://www.nalboh.org/).

Brandi Jessemy Whitney's job is to provide guidance to employers in the Atlanta area who have limited resources for wellness initiatives. As the health promotion coordinator for the Office of

Chronic Disease Prevention for the DeKalb County Board of Health, Georgia, Whitney's goal is to help companies develop sustainable policies, not just occasional programs. "We ask them: What do they envision? What is their goal? What policies will support healthy lifestyles? How to they see implementing their goals?" Whitney then helps them develop policies based on their answers and works with them, and "we show them how to do it on a reduced budget, how to bring in key partners."

Boards of health and business organizations in some communities work together to sponsor a local wellness council. The Wellness Council of America (WELCOA) has more than 3,200 member organizations around the country. WELCOA, based in Omaha, Nebraska, helps business leaders, workplace wellness practitioners, public health professionals, and consultants build "Well Workplaces." Information about publications, training, and WELCOA's Well Workplace Awards is available at http://www.welcoa.org/.

There are plenty of great services available at the local level, says Lisa Henning, executive director of WorkWell, the Lincoln-Lancaster, Nebraska, wellness council. "I have nurses, specialists. There are lots of good private resources that offer heath appraisals and services. . . . If a company in a small town in Nebraska wants to get started with a wellness program, I can help them get started in the right way."

WorkWell offers turnkey resources, a train the trainer program, tools such as survey instruments and consulting and a network so that company representatives can learn from each other. When a company calls, asking what it can do to get started, Henning responds with questions of her own: Does the company have a wellness champion in a top leadership position? Is there a wellness team? Has the company collected data on what employees need and want? "Too many companies play Russian roulette wellness—they just offer something; they don't know what people want or need," she says. After looking at the data, she urges the company to put its plan in writing, "even if it's half a page" and then to measure the changes in the workplace.

Wellness councils work with the local medical community as well as with employers, Henning says. "We're not trying to replace physicians. We just want to be sure people are in a good relationship with their physicians, not practicing medicine themselves. We're trying to educate the client, so that the person is well informed when he or she go to physician's office and has 4.3 minutes with the doctor. There's not a lot of time [for the physician] to look at the patient's history, to be thorough, so we to do some education with individuals."

THE BOTTOM LINE

You don't have to do all the work yourself to keep employees healthy and productive. Hospitals and insurance companies have a vested interest in preventive medicine and will work with you to offer educational programs, coaching, and screenings. The right insurance broker can help you find the right health plan. You also can turn to wellness councils and state and local boards of health to help stretch your limited budget.

By now you realize that when it comes to wellness, one size doesn't fit all. Chapter 10 deals with tailoring programs to meet the diverse needs of your particular workforce.

Profile: The Community Steps Up (http://www.co.ellis.tx.us)

It may not take a village to sustain a wellness initiative, but it helps. When Diana Buckley, director of human resources for Ellis County, Texas, added wellness to her weighty list of responsibilities, she turned to partners in the community to lighten her load. The community responded.

When Buckley was directed to put together a wellness initiative for 550 county employees and their families, the impetus was cost. Workers' compensation premiums had doubled, and "that big-dollar ticket item got the attention" and buy-in from the elected local governing board, Buckley says.

Brainstorming sessions resulted in the realization that "health and safety are inseparable. Employees who are healthy and thinking about their health are also safe and thinking about their safety," she says. The plan, then, was to create a single program to address the costs of health insurance and sick leave but also workers' comp insurance.

First up on the agenda was "payroll propaganda"—flyers on a variety of timely health and safety topics that were included "with each and every paycheck each and every payday." That's when neighboring organizations started becoming partners.

Texas AgriLife Extension Services, a statewide agency, agreed to provide the handouts at no charge, folded and ready to go. "They are educators and so it was right up their alley to volunteer," Buckley says, adding that the agency's wellness advice was reliable and research-based. The initial payroll propaganda flyer came out in summertime and since "we live in sun country," it addressed sun safety. "Four people told me they went to the dermatologist because they saw the flyer."

Then Buckley organized a health fair with 40 exhibitors from the community at a facility provided by Ellis County Youth Expo. One of two local hospitals, Baylor Medical Center Waxahachie, provided free glucose and cholesterol testing.

With her limited budget (about $3,000), she purchased mugs, mouse pads, glasses keepers, magnets, and water bottles imprinted with the health fair logo to use as incentives to get employees to answer surveys about educational programs they would like to attend and about the best times and places for holding classes. Employees work at various locations around the county and some work nights.

For the first class, Buckley brought in a doctor from a local clinic to talk about blood pressure. An employee from the Division of Workers Compensation taught defensive driving, Texas AgriLife Extension Services gave a lesson on basic nutrition, and a county employee who is a Red Cross volunteer taught a CPR certification class.

When word got out about the classes, "we started receiving calls from others in the community," Buckley reports. A financial planning agent asked to sponsor a program and a personal trainer's organization taught a class on "the workplace workout." In return, speakers were and are permitted to distribute information about the products and services they sell.

Recognizing that wellness doesn't have to be a serious subject, Buckley is planning a comedy improv class to teach about stress reduction.

Many speakers provide employees with a healthy snack or meal. If not, "we buy food at the grocery store and prepare it ourselves."

A PARTNERSHIP IS BORN

When Bradley Mabry, director of business development for nearby Ennis Regional Medical Center, stopped by a county office to pay property taxes, another partnership was born.

Buckley recently had sent out memos explaining that colonoscopy screenings were covered 100 percent by the county's health insurer, but one employee had received a bill from the anesthesiologist. "I mentioned the problem to [Mabry]. He called and said, 'How can we help?'" That led to more discussions, and Buckley says the hospital was "thrilled to learn that we would allow them to bring doctors, especially those new to the community, to teach health and safety classes to our employees."

The hospital also offered to identify the various preventive screening programs that were covered under employees' insurance plan at little or no cost. Insurance is difficult to navigate, and it pays to have someone savvy enough to know how it works and is willing to do the homework, says Mabry. "We've been able to explain to [Buckley] where the value is in this, and Diana did a good job of letting us do our job. We do the homework, because the hospital wants the business. We say, 'let us be a good steward.' They've engaged us to do what we can to offer resources and develop programs that will be beneficial for the county and the hospital."

Reaching out for help from the community has paid off, Buckley reports. "We had been told all year that our workers' comp premiums would go up again before they would start down no matter what we did, but in the end, we were successful enough to actually have a 3 percent decrease in our workers comp premiums for 2009—approximately $20,000, which is more than we have spent on the program."

When an organization has to concentrate on the bottom line, "usually it means you're offering less for your employees. This is case where by offering them more and treating them better, we're actually improving their quality of life and improving the bottom line," Buckley says.

Chapter Ten

No Size Fits All

While experts can argue over whether it's more effective to reach the sickest or the healthiest people, there's no debate that men and women of all ages and all racial, ethnic, and socioeconomic groups deserve equal access to wellness programs. You will want to recognize the special needs within your own workforce and address them, but you may not give one specific group a benefit that isn't available to everyone.

With justifiable concerns about discrimination against minorities, is it legal even to collect and share data on health-care quality by race and ethnicity? Yes, says a George Washington University policy brief. No federal or state liability exists for health-care providers "as long as the effort is part of an overall quality improvement process. In fact, experts agree, the use of data to improve quality and reduce disparities may decrease the risk of 'race-based' malpractice claims."[1]

Employees are free to volunteer information through enrollment forms and health assessments. If your organization has affinity or employee resource groups for various minorities, they can be useful for gathering data and delivering information. "The people on the distribution list for these groups have chosen to be on it," says Andrés Tapia, chief diversity officer for Hewitt Associates in Lincolnshire, Illinois. "Employers can work with those leaders to increase participation," notes Tapia.

Even with accurate data on demographics, take extra care in crafting appropriate messages for different groups. Some cultures have a fatalistic view of health and won't be moved to act simply by seeing a face similar to theirs on a flier, says Tapia. Appealing to their sense of family or other cultural stimuli may better motivate them to take action on health-care needs.[2]

AGE-OLD ISSUES

Older workers are a substantial—and growing—segment of the working population. By 2016, one in three workers will be 50 and older, according to U.S. Bureau of Labor Statistics projections.

While the aging of the workforce should raise health concerns, don't assume the news is all bad. Workers in their sixties are far more attentive to their health than those in their thirties, and employees over 50 take better care of themselves with regard to level of exercise, outlook on life, social support, and stress levels. That's the word from ComPsych Corporation. Other findings from the ComPsych study include the following:

- Of employees in their sixties, 52.2 percent had healthy diets, compared to 17.7 percent of workers in their thirties.
- Of employees in their fifties, 27.3 percent exercised more than four days a week, while 19.6 percent of thirtysomething workers did so.
- Of workers in their sixties, 82.6 percent had a very positive outlook on life, compared to 46 percent of employees in their thirties.
- Of employees in their sixties, 30.4 percent had high stress levels, while 64.7 percent of thirtysomethings had high stress.

The finding that employees in their thirties "were remarkably inactive," may be due, in part, to the fact that they are more likely to be consumed with raising a family and aren't allocating the time for exercise, says Dr. Richard A. Chaifetz, chairman and CEO of ComPsych, which is based in Chicago.

Workers "in their thirties may be at peak productivity but they also are at greatest risk for neglecting their health and developing long-term health problems due to poor lifestyle choices," adds Chaifetz, so "corporate wellness programs should be especially attentive to the needs and issues of this age group."[3]

Seeing the same types of problems with young workers is Fred Goldstein, president and CEO of Dallas-based U.S. Preventive Medicine. "We're beginning to see cardiac and lifestyle issues in this [thirtysomething] age group," he says. There is a reluctance to take part in health initiatives "because their lives are getting in the way.

They're figuring out how to get kids to school [and] make time for work, home and friends; that's all feeding a more sedentary lifestyle." Plus, younger workers' health issues aren't pressing yet, and "you don't focus on your health until there's a problem."[4]

To engage younger workers in wellness activities, it can help to emphasize the importance of exercise as a family activity and of obesity as a risk factor for their children as well as themselves. It certainly helps to give such employees access to work/life programs that help with child care and elder care.

Communicating with younger workers is most effective using technology. Gen Xers—people born between 1965 and 1976—tend to trust the medical community overall. They communicate 24/7 via mobile phone and prefer health information that is readily available, interactive, and fun, according to a study by Gordian Health Solutions. Gen Yers—those born between 1979 and 1999—seek "health content mainly out of curiosity. They are impatient and crave positive feedback and validation. For the Gen Y generation, health coaching programs" should be available around the clock and be easy to use and fun.

The Boomer generation—defined as people born between 1946 and 1964—tends to be wary of online health services due to concerns about privacy, according to a study by Gordian Health Solutions. But Boomers still value online health content. The Gordian study found that people 65 and older are not afraid of going on the Internet but are concerned about the accuracy of the information.[5]

LifeCare Inc., an employee benefits organization in Shelton, Connecticut, polled older workers and developed tips for better communication:

- Sixty-seven percent of older workers said they felt that achieving a healthy lifestyle is more difficult as they get older, so LifeCare recommends sending messages that talk about incremental, achievable changes.
- Ninety-four percent of older workers said they realize they must eat a healthier diet, but 37 percent expressed confusion about what that means, so it's important to make message about healthy eating clear and easy to understand.
- The majority of older workers want to be individualistic, so LifeCare recommends messages to them that reinforce that individuality.

- Sixty-seven percent of older workers say their top concern is financial health, according to LifeCare, so link your health messages to your financial benefits.[6]

X AND Y FACTORS

Whether your workforce is predominately male or female obviously makes a difference in which diseases you target with your wellness programs. A mostly male workforce means more education and screening for prostate cancer, while a predominately female workforce means greater concentration on such things as mammograms and prenatal care.

Mental wellness is a big factor here. Women are about twice as likely as men to suffer from major depression and chronic mild depression, known as dysthymia,[7] with women of child-bearing age and women of color especially at risk. Depression in women is misdiagnosed 30 percent to 50 percent of the time. Approximately 70 percent of the prescriptions for antidepressants are given to women, often with improper diagnosis and monitoring.[8]

The good news is that women are more likely to seek out help from Employee Assistance Programs. A six-month study of utilization trends by found that 63 percent of the callers to the EAP were female, and 37 percent of the callers were male, according to Bensinger, DuPont & Associates (BDA), a national Employee Assistance Program provider.

Women comprise 46 percent of the total U.S. labor force, according to the U.S. Department of Labor, yet they make significantly more calls to the EAP. Women use EAP services "more than males at almost a 3 to 1 ratio," notes Gus Stieber, of Bensinger DuPont & Associates. While it's not clear why this happens, he says, "one explanation is that, overall, research has shown women are more likely than men to seek help for concerns related to mental health and well-being—which are the traditional issues handled by EAPs."[9]

CURING MALE SYNDROME

The word on the men in your workplace is that they tend to suffer from *male syndrome,* a reluctance to use the health-care system.

"They're not good at going to see a doctor. They're not good at taking control of their health care," says Craig Johnson, wellness and safety manager for Duncan Aviation in Lincoln, Nebraska. Johnson knows a lot about the syndrome—about 90 percent of Duncan's 2,200 employees in Lincoln and Battle Creek, Michigan, are male.

The WELCOA Platinum Award–winning company tried offering voluntary lunch and learn sessions, says Johnson, but "that was getting less than one percent [of the workers] and none of them were high risk." His solution was to require quarterly health education sessions on-site—on company time. "They weren't going to do it voluntarily but because it's at work and it's free, we removed every barrier. I would argue that that would be smart approach for anyone."

The company makes good use of the expertise of its on-site wellness staff, requiring each manager to invite a staff person to speak once per quarter during a regularly scheduled meeting. The required meetings have been a culture changer at Duncan, Johnson says, because "it's in a setting where it doesn't feel like we're forcing it down their throat. We've become a familiar face and [are] able to break down their reluctance."

Wellness staff members should want to see themselves as employee resources and make it a goal to be in high demand, he adds. "You shouldn't be able to walk through the shop without people coming up to you and asking questions. It gives you good job security, it means people are demanding your services."

Early on, the company's educational sessions were generic, but the wellness staff has learned to customize information to the needs of each department. The wellness staff stays attuned to the particular preferences of its workforce in other ways as well. Duncan hasn't put much wellness information on line because "that doesn't appear to be what our people want. They love it face to face," Johnson says.

DISPROPORTIONATE PROBLEMS

Statistics show that members of minority groups—regardless of income, insurance status, or community of residence—aren't as healthy as their Caucasian counterparts.

African Americans, who represent 13 percent of the U.S. population, are disproportionally affected by certain diseases, including HIV/AIDS, cancer, heart disease, and stroke, according to statistics from the Centers for Disease Control and Prevention. They have higher rates of obesity and are four times more likely to get diabetes than non-Hispanic whites.

African Americans trailed Caucasians in four positive health indicators: having health insurance coverage (81% of non-Hispanic blacks vs. 87% of non-Hispanic whites); taking flu vaccine (50% vs. 69%); receiving prenatal care in the first trimester of pregnancy (75% vs. 89%); and participating in regular, moderate physical activity (25% vs. 35%), the CDC reports.[10]

The unique cancer risks faced by Hispanic Americans requires an approach to prevention and treatment geared to their special needs, notes the American Cancer Society. While Hispanic Americans are less likely than non-Hispanic Caucasians to develop and die from the most common cancers (female breast, prostate, colorectal, and lung), they do have higher rates of several types of cancers related to infectious agents, including cancers of the stomach, liver, and cervix, as well as gallbladder, and acute lymphocytic leukemia.

Hispanics are more likely to have cancer detected at a later stage than non-Hispanic Caucasians, according to an American Cancer Society report, and they have lower survival rates for most cancers, even after accounting for differences in age and stage at diagnosis. They are less likely to be screened for female breast, cervical, colorectal, and prostate cancers and are more likely to be diagnosed at a later stage for cancers of the lung, colon and rectum, prostate, female breast, and skin. Hispanics also are more likely to be overweight or obese, factors that are associated with cancer risk, according to the American Cancer Society report.

Obviously some of the approaches that are most important in your overall population also are important to Hispanics. That includes giving employees access to screenings and appropriate follow-up care, encouraging them to be physically active and to maintain a healthy body weight, and preventing and treating tobacco dependence.

But beyond that, the keys to helping Hispanics stay healthy are to remove language and cultural barriers that interfere with access to high-quality screening and medical care, and to work at forming partnerships to deliver your health messages more effectively, according to Dr. Michael J. Thun, vice president, epidemiological and surveillance research for the American Cancer Society.[11]

Language can be a barrier to wellness. Approximately 1 in 8 Americans were born in another country, and 52 million Americans speak a language other than English at home, according to the Census Bureau. If your workforce has nonnative English speakers, you'll want to make efforts to provide programs in their languages.

LACK OF TRUST

Lack of cultural understanding is yet another barrier, says Dr. Elena V. Rios, president and CEO of the National Hispanic Medical Association and president of the National Hispanic Medical Foundation. The overall low education attainment of Hispanics means there are few Hispanic health-care professionals, she notes, causing some people to call for teaching non-Hispanics how to work effectively with Latino patients in cross-cultural situations. For example, Rios says, non-Hispanic health professionals must understand the effect on health-care deliberations that can emerge from the connectedness of Latinos—the extended family, including godparents and close friends.[12]

A lack of understanding can lead to a lack of trust in the health-care system as a whole. Seventy percent of minority women surveyed by Michigan State University indicated they do not use health-related screening tests because they believe that medical providers sometimes mislead or deceive patients. Suspicions about care may mean that people are less likely to receive preventive screenings, says Karen Patricia Williams, the study's lead author and assistant professor of obstetrics, gynecology, and reproductive biology at Michigan State. That makes it less likely that they will be diagnosed early with conditions that might have been effectively treated.

The study of Arab American, African American, and Hispanic women found that African Americans were the most mistrustful of the health-care system, with 39 percent distrusting health-care organizations, compared to 15 percent of Hispanics, and 9 percent of Arab American women. Overall, 44 percent of minority women who have never had a breast examination said they believed that health-care organizations sometimes performed harmful experiments on patients without their consent.[13]

REDUCING THE DISPARITY

Health-insurers are well aware of the disparities, and some are taking steps to improve health care for various groups. The National Committee for Quality Assurance has honored a number of managed care plans for their innovative programs:

- Aetna—African Americans' higher prevalence of hypertension led to development of a Culturally Competent Disease Management Program (CCDMP) that included educational mailing kits and personalized outreach from disease management nurses for participants, plus quarterly reports for the patients' primary care physicians. Compared to a control group receiving a lightly managed program without a cultural focus, CCDMP members had a higher percentage of members with clinically acceptable blood pressures, and there was an increase in blood pressure monitoring and medication usage.

- Highmark Inc. (Pennsylvania)—A partnership with SilverSneakers Fitness Program included fitness memberships as part of the total benefit coverage to empower Medicare Advantage members to adopt a regular fitness routine. However, African Americans' participation was far lower than that of Caucasians. Through gap analysis, enhanced marketing materials, targeted staff training and community outreach, Highmark saw participation increase from 3.4 percent to 18 percent in four years, exceeding that of Caucasians members.

- Keystone Mercy Health Plan (Pennsylvania)—A community- and faith-based wellness program offered participants access to health screenings, healthy eating education, stress management, and even Gospel aerobics. Participants lost weight, improved their mobility and flexibility, and lowered their heart rate and blood pressure.

- Molina Healthcare of Michigan—In 2006, only 7 percent of African American males in Detroit received preventive health exams. The "Check Up or Check Out!" program was designed to address the underutilization of preventive health-care services among African American males. Through personal outreach, education and incentives, preventive exam rates increased from 7 percent to 19 percent, while testing rates for cholesterol, glucose, colorectal and prostate cancer doubled.

- UnitedHealthcare (New York)—Chinese-speaking seniors (including those eligible for Medicaid and Medicare services) were disenrolling as a result of cultural and linguistic barriers. Oxford Health Plan developed in-language walk-in centers to help seniors apply for Medicaid and other social service and community health programs. As a result, more members received benefits and disenrollment was halved.

- UnitedHealthcare Latino Health Solutions—An "Enhanced Bilingual Service and Member Access Initiative" was designed to improve Spanish-speaking members' interactions with the plan. Through cultural training and phone routing to Spanish-speaking customer care professionals (CCPs), satisfaction among members using CCPs increased from 65 percent to 90 percent.

- Virginia Premier Health Plan Inc.—African American women members were half as likely to breast-feed as Caucasian members before initiation of a breast-feeding collaboration with the Virginia Department of Medical Assistance Services and other community agencies. Through education and support—such as classes, hotlines, peer support groups, lactation consultants, and free breast pumps—breast-feeding rates increased from 22 percent to 51 percent.

- Wellpoint Inc.—To overcome a lack of self-reported race and ethnicity membership information, a means to indirectly derive information was developed with support from RAND Corporation. The resulting data enabled comparison of health plan performance by race and ethnic group. Overlaying the performance data with geographic software produced maps showing health disparity "hotspots," supporting planning for improved service and access.[14] The Program is funded by The California Endowment and is supported by the Centers for Medicare & Medicaid Services and The Office of Minority Health.

> *Source:* National Committee for Quality Assurance,
> "Innovative Practices in Multicultural Health Care,"
> 2008. Reprinted with permission.

ACCESS FOR ALL

Don't forget about the people in your workplace who have disabilities. Reasonable accommodations that give them access to wellness programs will pay off in the long run.

In fact, integrating accessibility into all employer-sponsored health and wellness activities increases the productivity of the entire workforce, not only employees with disabilities, notes Eileen Elias, former deputy director of the Department of Health and Human Services' Office of Disability and now senior policy advisor for Disability and Mental Health, for JBS International Inc.[15]

Ensure accessible design from the outset by including employees with disabilities in the creation, development, and design of your wellness programs and services. Include accessible health and wellness language in your company's mission statement. Put together a checklist for managers and vendors to remind them that programs offered internally or purchased should be designed to be available to all eligible users.

New Editions Consulting Inc., in McLean, Virginia, provides program management, research, evaluation, and technical assistance on health, disability, and social policy. About one-third of the small company's employees have disabilities, and the company allows a flexible work schedule and teleworking to accommodate transportation needs and scheduling for doctor or other health-care appointments. It also offer a flexible spending plan to help employees who have special health-care needs that most plans don't cover.

When New Editions planned a company-wide event as part of a national "Walk at Lunch Day," planners made sure the route would be accessible to employees who use wheelchairs, turning it into "Walk/Roll at Lunch Day," according to President Shelia Newman. "Everything we do teaches us more about what we can do—and improves all team members' commitment to the organization. We all benefit from that," Newman says.

INDUSTRY DIFFERENCES

How you approach your wellness program depends not only on the age and ethnicity of your workforce, but the nature and number of your workplaces. Is yours a small business or a multinational corporation? Is everyone in one location, or do you have employees who work remotely? Which jobs are physically strenuous or unusually stressful?

What industry you're in can be a factor. Some industries are doing better at wellness program participation than others, based on a study by Gordian Health Solutions that looked at enrollment rates relative to the study population average. Here are the rates for major industries:

1. Healthcare and social assistance: 157 percent of the average
2. Food manufacturing: 151 percent
3. Other manufacturing: 104 percent
4. Professional/scientific/technical: 97 percent
5. Finance and insurance: 92 percent
6. Retail trade: 62 percent
7. Educational services: 60 percent
8. Information: 47 percent
9. Construction: 44 percent
10. Utilities: 22 percent

A unionized environment presents challenges as well because cost shifting, for the most part, is off the table. With limited ability to alter the plan design because it has been negotiated with the union, the real issue becomes preventing disease, says Dr. William B. Bunn, vice president for health, safety, security, and productivity at Navistar International Corp. Navistar is the holding company for International Truck & Engine Corp., where the workforce is 62 percent unionized, mostly through the United Auto Workers. "We have to influence health behavior, because we're not going to have a lot of cost-sharing kinds of strategies."

The company has a corporate wellness council and wellness teams in every operating site. Each local cross-plant team is made up of union and management volunteers and has an executive sponsor, usually the plant manager. "The local programs are picked by the site guys," according to Bunn. "They decide what they want to do over the course of this year to improve the health of the employees."

Participation has been increasing each year, due to local teams communicating the program and local plant management supporting their efforts, he says, noting the importance of support from both senior management and local unions. "If you can get support of the local union, you get a lot of support. It's top-down and bottom-up."[16]

Employees who work shifts, work remotely, or travel regularly can all benefit from good online wellness programs. Shift workers and transportation workers in particular face sleep and nutrition problems that probably will require you to modify parts of your programs accordingly. Such employees especially need education about healthy eating and about the role of sleep on overall health and immunity. Offer these employees informational sessions on nutrition, the importance of a regular sleep schedule, and dealing with daytime distractions that disturb sleep. Be sure you offer these programs at times that fit in with their schedule.

And what type of wellness program should you offer employees who work in call centers? Certainly not telephonic health coaching for workers who are on the telephone for hours at a time. Online wellness education would be a better bet.

Getting enough physical activity is a real challenge for call center employees, so one international company is considering piloting "walk stations," where they can exercise while they're working. The plan is to sign employees up for turns on the limited number of stations.

GROWING GLOBALLY

Workplace wellness initiatives are growing rapidly in popularity around the world to the point where 40 percent of employers surveyed in Europe, Asia, and Africa now offer these programs. Wellness initiatives are still most prevalent in North America, with 82 percent of employers surveyed by Buck Consultants saying they offer them. Technology-driven tools, such as online programs, Web portals and personal health records, are the fastest-growing elements of wellness initiatives being used around the globe. Other wellness tools that are being used at a growing rate are health fairs, workplace health competition, and vending machines stocked with nutritious food choices. Buck Consultants predicts that use of these program components will grow dramatically—in some cases, by more than 100 percent in regions outside of North America.

The business objectives for wellness programs vary. In the United States health-care cost reduction continues to be the primary objective, while Canadian employers cite improving productivity as the top goal. European companies cite improving workforce morale as the main objective. Asian and African respondents cite reducing employee absence as their main goal.[17]

While you may have one overall wellness philosophy for your multinational company, the programs being offered in various countries should be carefully customized to fit the needs of local workers. You may try moving a wellness program that works fine at one location to another location, but if you ignore local cultural sensitivities, employees may resist the program before it ever starts, spoiling its chance of success, says Helen Darling, president of the National Business Group on Health (NBGH). To help U.S.-based companies implement wellness programs at overseas locations, NBGH has established a Global Health Benefits Institute.

Different diseases and conditions are of varying concern in difference countries. Obesity is a serious problem in many parts of the world, but other health problems are not so universal. Trying to curb employee smoking is seen mainly as a U.S. activity, with companies operating in Western Europe becoming more aware of the issue. In Southern Europe, South America, and Africa, trying to control employee smoking off the job is still seen as "crossing the boundary of what the employer can do," says Steven Bevan, executive director of The Work Foundation, based in London.

Mental health is another area where attitudes differ based on culture. In the United States and parts of Western Europe it is considered more acceptable "to blame what is making you [mentally] ill on external factors . . . people believe work can make them ill. You won't find that in the developing world such as India and parts of Africa," Bevan says.[18]

An added consideration for global companies is that there are not well-developed vendor markets in some parts of the world, making it more difficult to offer some types of wellness programs.

ON THE ROAD

Corning Inc., working with its international insurer Cigna International Expatriate Benefits, has developed a pilot program to encourage overseas-bound employees and their families to volunteer for its predeparture physical-exam program, designed to identify health issues prior to the assignment.

"We've taken a disease-management approach," says Dr. James Schuppert, director of health services at Corning, based in Corning, New York. "We identify what gaps there are before going on assignment."

The program takes into account chronic conditions, such as asthma, that could be aggravated by the environment where the family will be living. "If a child will be moving to Taiwan where there's more air pollution, we make sure he's well tuned up and on the right medications before they go," Schuppert says.[19]

PepsiCo, based in Purchase, New York, launched its employee wellness program, Healthroads, in the United States in the early 2000s. Since then it has implemented programs in Canada and the United Kingdom and is considering expanding to Australia.

In the United States, the backbone of PepsiCo's program is WebMD, an online health information service. In Canada, PepsiCo decided to stay with the WebMD Web site, but with Canadian-specific content and a French translation. As the company expands the program, it plans to ensure that different languages are part of the program where needed when the program is rolled out to various countries.

Among the specifics of the United States and Canadian program versions are that each employee who takes a voluntary health-risk assessment is assigned a coach who specializes in behavior change to work with the individual on specific health needs such as weight loss or smoking cessation.[20]

The company has overcome cultural barriers in the past, such as when it introduced its stock-option plan, but that didn't involve something as personal as people changing eating habits, for example, says David Scherb, PepsiCo's vice president of compensation and benefits. "We know it's not going to be easy. We might have to stop, backtrack and try another way." He believes moving the wellness plan into English- and Spanish-speaking countries will be less problematic than rolling it out into other countries where different languages could pose some difficulties. However, "if you think about how broadly we're defining our game, there's a universal link—our global brands—and being healthier and feeling better is a fairly universal thing."[21]

SMALL-SCALE WELLNESS

Given the numbers, it's quite likely that you're implementing a wellness initiative in a small-business setting. Small companies hire half of all private sector employees and pay more than 45 percent of the total U.S. private payroll, according to the Office of Advocacy of the U.S. Small Business Administration. If you are dealing with a small business, your company may lack the financial firepower of giant corporations, but there's still plenty you can do to help your employees get and stay healthy. Just adjust the scale.

Encourage physical activity. One of the easiest and cheapest ways for a small company to do that is by promoting walking. For a few dollars each, or perhaps free from your insurance provider, you can buy pedometers to pass out to your employees. They can keep track of the number of daily steps they take and work to increase the amount they exercise each day. Sponsoring a walking competition at work is a great way to build their enthusiasm for exercise.

Help employees choose nutritious food. You may not have a corporate cafeteria, but you can stock healthy food in your refrigerator or vending machine. Give employees facts about nutrition to help them make better decisions. Information about the nutritional content of fast-food is available on most chains' Web sites.[22]

Conduct a survey of employee interests, and have your CEO send out messages that encourage employees to take part in wellness activities. Give them opportunities for health screening, perhaps through local hospitals, so they can assess and understand their own personal health status.

Good health is based, at least in part on good information, so give your employees opportunities to learn more about prevention right at work. Ask local health experts to sponsor lunch-and-learn sessions and health fairs. Send out newsletters and, if it fits the needs and interests of your employees, provide Web-based tools. You might even establish an in-house lending library. Include medical self-care books, health magazines, instructional DVDs, and a variety of pamphlets. Again, ask local experts to supply materials. To make sure employees take advantage of all that information, it's a good idea to put the library in a commonly traveled spot.[23]

THE BOTTOM LINE

In your drive for a healthy, productive workforce, you can't afford to overlook any section of your population. Make sure you tailor your initiative to the size of your company and the diversity of your workforce. That diversity includes age, sex, race, ethnicity, and persons with disabilities. Don't forget about employees who work remotely or on overnight shifts. Whatever the size, location, and composition of your organization, make wellness at work for everyone.

What's Your Profile?

There is no profile for "The Ideal Company," because when it comes to wellness no single ideal exists. But by recognizing the needs and diversity of your workforce, you can create the wellness model that is right for your organization.

The first step is to arm yourself with the facts and to share them with top management. There's a strong case to be made that a properly designed wellness initiative can increase employees' health and productivity. Build a case that demonstrates how an effective program can save your organization money on medical expenditures and insurance costs—and reap productivity gains as well. Show the executive team how wellness can improve their own lives and how it can give your organization a competitive advantage over others in your industry.

Once you've convinced top management that wellness is worth it, it's time for them to promote it, model it, and champion it. Have executives communicate to employees how wellness fits into the business objective and improves their lives, and encourage them to walk the talk.

A wellness team or committee made up of representatives from throughout the organization is the best way to design and implement a well-thought-out program and handle employee feedback. Make sure team members know what they're getting into and—through surveys—make sure they know what employees want and need. Use your team to determine an overall strategy with clear objectives, and rely on team members to sell the program their peers. Have the team periodically evaluate your wellness program and, if necessary, make adjustments. And don't forget to reward your committee members for all their hard work.

With senior management onboard and a wellness team in place, pick some of that low-hanging fruit. Start with basic educational programs that provide workers with information about how to lead healthier lives and illustrate ways they can change those behaviors that are most likely to damage their health.

Encourage employees to eat healthier foods not only by providing information about nutrition, but by removing some of the temptations lurking in the company vending machines and cafeterias.

Help employees get and stay in good physical shape by sponsoring simple exercise programs that encourage them to be just a little more active each day. Walking is great exercise, and a step-counting program is one of the easiest ways to start people on the road to a more active life. Encourage running, swimming, biking. Offer classes and discounted gym memberships.

Use technology to prod people into taking action, and use it to share employee success stories. Inform, encourage, but don't preach.

Offer employees meaningful incentives to change their behavior. If you want your incentive plan to be successful—and legal—give all employees a chance to take part and focus on participation rather than on outcomes. An incentive given for taking part in a wellness activity, rather than for achieving a particular target or standard, generally is not discriminatory.

You can offer many types of incentives: small prizes, chances at big prizes, points that can be accumulated for prizes, or cash prizes. But the prize that delivers the wellness message most effectively is one that offers employees a rebate on their health insurance premiums when they take steps toward healthier behavior.

You might try disincentives, such as penalizing employees who smoke, but carrots work better than sticks and are more likely to be legal.

To get data about the wellness needs of your workforce, encourage employees to take comprehensive health assessments. Assessments identify the top health risks in your organization, but you have to get employees to take them. To convince them to take part in the assessment progress, show them how you are protecting their privacy, and offer them some type of incentive, preferably tied to their insurance premiums. You can require that employees take assessments, but the carrot is mightier than the stick.

The health assessment process is not just a matter of having employees fill out questionnaires. Include lab work and biometrics (the statistical analysis of biological phenomena), and follow up with coaching sessions. Set your expectations at the right level. A health assessment is a catalyst for a behavior change program; it's not a behavior change program of itself. Use the information you receive from assessments to build a stronger wellness program that addresses the specific risks your organization faces.

To help combat health risks more effectively, you might consider an on-site medical clinic and/or fitness center. Such facilities certainly make your employees' lives more convenient—and healthier—and your company can reap benefits as well. An on-site fitness center makes it easy for employees to get more exercise and to become and stay healthy. It can offer personalized instruction and even increase interaction among employees from various departments of your organization. An on-site health center promotes early medical intervention and treatment, which reduces the need for costly specialty care, emergency room usage, hospitalization and absence from work. If your company is small, consider joining with other organizations to provide these services.

Your employees' physical health shouldn't be your only concern. Their mental health is just as crucial, and mental illness certainly can be as costly as physical illness. You want at least to have an Employee Assistance Program (EAP), usually run by a third-party vendor, to help your employees identify and resolve personal problems relating to health, family, finances, addiction, and stress. A good EAP vendor provides your employees with confidential and timely problem identification, assessment, and counseling services and can refer employees to other health-care professionals for diagnosis, treatment, and assistance.

In addition to providing an EAP, look for ways your organization can come up with creative ways to reduce employee's stress and increase their productivity. Any programs that help them balance work and family obligations will go a long way toward meeting those goals. Offer opportunities for growth and development and recognize employee achievement.

Tap into community resources. Hospitals and insurance companies have a vested interest in preventive medicine and will work with you to offer educational programs, coaching, and screenings. The right insurance broker can help you find the right health plan. You also can turn to wellness councils and state and local boards of health to help stretch your limited budget.

Put it all together, and you've created a wellness profile that meets the specific needs of your workers and your company.

Appendix A

The Awards

C. EVERETT KOOP NATIONAL HEALTH AWARDS
(HTTP://WWW.SPH.EMORY.EDU/HEALTHPROJECT/)

Any program that believes it may be competitive may apply without having been nominated. Nominations (as opposed to applications) are sought from all Health Project and Task Force members. Nominations need only include the name of the program, contact person, address, phone and fax numbers, and an e-mail address if possible. Programs will be responsible for application development.

The Program Nomination Task Force will systematically develop additional nominations. The task force has added a category of "Web-enabled" and hopes to be able to make awards in this category. The task force would also like to receive applications from programs that have improved health and resulted in quantifiable productivity increases.

The goal is to be able to recognize any program of whatever type or source that can document true cost savings from health risk improvements and demand reduction. Previous winners are eligible except for the year immediately following the award and will be judged on the basis of all available documentation. However, to be considered, a previous winner must present and document some additional new data on their program's effectiveness and cost savings since the prior application.

Categories (programs may be in more than one) include chronic disease, community, government, high risk, innovator/vendor, insurance, integrated systems of care, low birth weight babies, Web-enabled, productivity enhancing, and worksite based.

Applicant programs are required to send 15 copies of the application to the Program Selection Task Force Chair. Evaluation will be by the Program Selection Task Force, augmented by members of the Program Nomination Task Force, in three stages. First, primary and secondary reviewers with appropriate experience will screen candidate programs for those deserving full evaluation, selecting those believed potentially to be serious candidates for the awards. Second, the full Task Force of 12 reviewers will review and score all screened programs. Third, the Executive Committee will review and approve final awards at its meeting in August.

Please indicate your intent to apply by sending an e-mail with your contact information to healthproject@emory.edu. Fifteen copies of an application must be submitted by mail, and one electronic application must be submitted. To request an application, contact healthproject@emory.edu. When requesting an application, make sure to include a contact name, the name of the company or organization that will be submitting the application, the full mailing address, telephone and fax numbers, and contact e-mail address.

Ron Z. Goetzel, Ph.D.
Chairman, Program Selection Task Force
Emory University
Institute for Health and Productivity Studies
1341 22nd Street NW
Washington, D.C. 20037

*Reprinted with permission of the National Health Awards.

NATIONAL BUSINESS GROUP ON HEALTH (HTTP:// WWW.BUSINESSGROUPHEALTH.ORG) BEST EMPLOYERS FOR HEALTHY LIFESTYLES AWARDS

The Best Employers for Healthy Lifestyles Award acknowledges and rewards those organizations that apply creative, comprehensive solutions to improving the health of employees; however, its most important purpose is to serve as a catalyst for action.

Confidentiality

The National Business Group on Health (NBGH) takes steps to protect company information provided in the Best Employers for Healthy Lifestyles applications. NBGH intends for company-specific data and information about company programs to be used for judging purposes only; judges agree to this before reviewing applications. Identified information (naming company programs) may not be shared without the consent of the applying company.

Eligibility

The Best Employers for Healthy Lifestyles Award is open exclusively to members of the National Business Group on Health.

Application Evaluation

Multiple reviewers with relevant experience will be assigned to each application.

Levels of Achievement

Platinum: Award reserved for organizations with mature "healthy weight, healthy lifestyles" programs and cultures. Financial and/ or nonfinancial measures of program performance are defined, and results are reported. If ROI is a stated metric, the results of the analysis are required with methods and assumptions explained. Programs have been fully operational for a minimum of three to five years and continue to innovate and improve based on analysis of their own data and experience. Case studies must accompany Platinum applications.

Gold: Awarded to organizations that are creating cultural and environmental changes to support employees who are making a commitment to long-term behavioral change. Healthy dining and physical activity are thoroughly addressed. A variety of communication channels, programs, and incentives reach employees (and families) throughout the organization; all Silver requirements have been met.

Silver: Awarded to organizations that have obtained high-level executive support, selected a dedicated steering committee or team to advance initiatives, undertaken health risk assessment or claims analyses to capture population-specific data, and launched programs or services supporting healthy weight, healthy lifestyles. Pilot programs are not eligible.

Overview of the Application

This application includes six (6) required sections and one optional addendum, required only for companies applying at the Platinum level.

Part I. Summary of your program, including key elements, innovative features, and effective practices.

Part II. Structure/Strategy—What is your company's "game plan" to encourage healthy lifestyles for employees and families?

Part III. Communications—Describe your communication channels and messages.

Part IV. Healthy Environment—Describe programs to improve healthy dining and increase physical activity.

Part V. HRA/Benefits—How is the HRA used to guide your program? How does your plan design support wellness?

Part VI. Results and Outcomes—What results and outcomes can you demonstrate?

*Reprinted with permission of the National Business Group on Health

PSYCHOLOGICALLY HEALTHY WORKPLACE AWARDS (HTTP://WWW.PHWA.ORG)

The Psychologically Healthy Workplace Awards are designed to recognize organizations for their efforts to foster employee health and well-being while enhancing organizational performance.

The Local Psychologically Healthy Workplace Award

Since 1999, Psychologically Healthy Workplace Awards have been presented to organizations by state, provincial, and territorial psychological associations with support from the American Psychological Association. The award program highlights a variety of workplaces, large and small, profit and nonprofit, in diverse geographical settings. Applicants are evaluated on their efforts in the following five areas:

- Employee Involvement
- Work-Life Balance
- Employee Growth and Development
- Health and Safety
- Employee Recognition

The local award program has been extremely successful, with participation growing to 52 associations across the United States and

Canada. Collectively, more than more than 400 organizations have been recognized at the state level.

APA's National Psychologically Healthy Workplace Award

The American Psychological Association presented its first annual National Psychologically Healthy Workplace Awards in March 2006. Nominees for the National Psychologically Healthy Workplace Award are selected from the pool of previous local winners. Following a competitive evaluation and judging process, the top candidates are selected for recognition by the American Psychological Association.

APA's Best Practice Honors

In 2003, the American Psychological Association launched the Best Practices Honors, a national recognition that highlights the efforts of those local winners with particularly innovative programs and policies that contribute to a psychologically healthy work environment.

As with the National Award, nominees come from the pool of previous local winners and are selected through a competitive evaluation and judging process.

*Reprinted with the permission of the American Psychological Association. For more information about the Psychologically Healthy Workplace Program, visit www.ohwa.org.

Sample Wellness Program Invitation from the CEO

To: Name of Employee
From: Chief Executive Officer

We're all worried about the high cost of health care, but together, in a partnership between the company and employees, we can do something about this significant problem. To prove we are strongly committed to the health of our organization and the health of our employees, we are introducing new wellness initiatives to help you achieve better health and keep it.

To kick off our wellness efforts, we will have [introduce event]. I have asked our [wellness committee chair] to seek employee feedback on our efforts. Please feel free to contact [him/her] with any suggestions on how we can continue to support you.

Members of the wellness committee include: [insert committee member names here].

I personally plan to take part in our wellness program and hope you will join me.

Appendix C

EBSA Wellness Program Analysis

U.S. Department of Labor
Employee Benefits Security Administration
Washington, D.C. 20210

FIELD ASSISTANCE BULLETIN NO. 2008-02

DATE: FEBRUARY 14, 2008

MEMORANDUM FOR: VIRGINIA C. SMITH, DIRECTOR OF ENFORCEMENT REGIONAL DIRECTORS

FROM: DANIEL J. MAGUIRE

DIRECTOR OF HEALTH PLAN STANDARDS AND COMPLIANCE ASSISTANCE

SUBJECT: WELLNESS PROGRAM ANALYSIS

ISSUE: What types of health promotion or disease prevention programs offered by a group health plan must comply with the Department's final wellness program regulations and how does a plan determine whether such a program is in compliance with the regulations?

BACKGROUND: On December 13, 2006, the Departments of Labor, the Treasury, and Health and Human Services published joint final regulations on the nondiscrimination provisions of the Health Insurance Portability and Accountability Act (HIPAA). *See* 29 CFR 2590.702. The final regulations include guidance on the implementation of wellness programs. HIPAA's nondiscrimination provisions generally prohibit a group health plan or group health insurance issuer from denying an individual eligibility for benefits based on a health factor and from charging an individual a higher premium than a similarly situated individual based on a health factor. Health factors include: health status, medical condition (including both physical and mental illnesses), claims experience, receipt of health care, medical history, genetic information, evidence of insurability (including conditions arising out of acts of domestic violence), and disability. An exception provides that plans may vary benefits (including cost-sharing mechanisms) and premiums or contributions based on whether an individual has met the standards of a wellness program that complies with paragraph (f) of the regulations.

The regulations apply to group health plans and group health insurance issuers on the first day of the plan year beginning on or after July 1, 2007. Accordingly, for calendar year plans, the new regulations began to apply on January 1, 2008. Since the issuance of the final regulations, the Department has received questions concerning what types of programs must comply with the standards of 29 CFR 2590.702(f) and how to apply these standards to particular well-ness programs. The following checklist provides further guidance.

WELLNESS PROGRAM CHECKLIST: Use the following questions to help determine whether the plan offers a program of health promotion or disease prevention that is required to comply with the Department's final wellness program regulations and, if so, whether the program is in compliance with the regulations.

A. Insert the first day of the current plan year: _____.

Is the date after July 1, 2007?   Yes   No

The wellness program final rules are applicable for plan years beginning on or after July 1, 2007.

B. Does the plan have a wellness program?   Yes   No

A wide range of wellness programs exist to promote health and prevent disease.

However, these programs are not always labeled "wellness programs." Examples include: a program that reduces individual's cost-sharing for complying with a preventive care plan; a diagnostic testing program for health problems; and rewards for attending educational classes, following healthy lifestyle recommendations, or meeting certain biometric targets (such as weight, cholesterol, nicotine use, or blood pressure targets).

TIP: Ignore the labels—wellness programs can be called many things. Other common names include: disease management programs, smoking cessation programs, and case management programs.

C. Is the wellness program part of a group health plan?
Yes   No

The wellness program is only subject to Part 7 of ERISA if it is part of a group health plan. If the employer operates the wellness program as an employment policy separate from the group health plan, the program may be covered by other laws, but it is not subject to the group health plan rules discussed here.

Example: An employer institutes a policy that any employee who smokes will be fired. Here, the plan is not acting, so the wellness program rules do not apply. (*But see* 29 CFR 2590.702, which clarifies that compliance with the HIPAA nondiscrimination rules, including the wellness program rules, is not determinative of compliance with any other provision of ERISA or any other State or Federal law, such as the Americans with Disabilities Act.)

D. Does the program discriminate based on a health factor?
Yes   No

A plan discriminates based on a health factor if it requires an individual to meet a standard related to a health factor in order to obtain a reward. A reward can be in the form of a discount or rebate of a premium or contribution, a waiver of all or part of a cost-sharing mechanism (such as deductibles, copayments, or coinsurance), the absence of a surcharge, or the value of a benefit that would otherwise not be provided under the plan.

Example 1: Plan participants who have a cholesterol level under 200 will receive a premium reduction of 20%. In this Example 1, the plan requires individuals to meet a standard related to a health factor in order to obtain a reward.

Example 2: A plan requires all eligible employees to complete a health risk assessment to enroll in the plan. Employee answers are fed into a computer that identifies risk factors and sends educational information to the employee's home address. In this Example 2, the requirement to complete the assessment does not, itself, discriminate based on a health factor. However, if the plan used individuals' specific health information to discriminate in individual eligibility, benefits, or premiums, there would be discrimination based on a health factor.

If you answered "**No**" to **ANY** of the above questions, **STOP.** The plan does not maintain a program subject to the group health plan wellness program rules.

E. If the program discriminates based on a health factor, is the program saved by the benign discrimination provisions?   Yes   No

The Department's regulations at 29 CFR 2590.702(g) permit discrimination *in favor* of an individual based on a health factor.

Example: Plan grants participants who have diabetes a waiver of the plan's annual deductible if they enroll in a disease management program that consists of attending educational classes and following their doctor's recommendations regarding exercise and medication. *This is benign discrimination because the program is offering a reward to individuals based on an adverse health factor.*

TIP: The benign discrimination exception is **NOT** available if the plan asks diabetics to meet a standard related to a health factor (such as maintaining a certain BMI) in order to get a reward. In this case, an *intervening discrimination* is introduced and the plan cannot rely solely on the benign discrimination exception.

If you answered "Yes" to the previous question, **STOP.** There are no violations of the wellness program rules.

If you answered "No" to the previous question, the wellness program must meet the following 5 criteria.

F. Compliance Criteria
(1) Is the amount of the reward offered under the plan limited to 20% of the applicable cost of coverage? (29 CFR 2590.702(f)(2)(i))   Yes   No

Keep in mind these considerations when analyzing the reward amount:

Who is eligible to participate in the wellness program?

If only employees are eligible to participate, the amount of the reward must not exceed 20% of the cost of employee-only coverage under the plan. If employees and any class of dependents are eligible to participate, the reward must not exceed 20% of the cost of coverage in which an employee and any dependents are enrolled.

Does the plan have more than one wellness program?

The 20% limitation on the amount of the reward applies to all of a plan's wellness programs *that require individuals to meet a standard related to a health factor.*

Example: If the plan has two wellness programs with standards related to a health factor, a 20% reward for meeting a body mass index target and a 10% reward for meeting a cholesterol target, it must decrease the total reward available from 30% to 20%. However, if instead, the program offered a 10% reward for meeting a body mass index target, a 10% reward for meeting a cholesterol target, and a 10% reward for completing a health risk assessment (regardless of any individual's specific health information), the rewards do not need to be adjusted because the 10% reward for completing the health risk assessment does not require individuals to meet a standard related to a health factor.

(2) Is the plan reasonably designed to promote health or prevent disease? (29 CFR 2590.702(f)(2)(ii))   Yes   No

The program must be reasonably designed to promote health or prevent disease. The program should have a reasonable chance of improving the health of or preventing disease in participating individuals, not be overly burdensome, not be a subterfuge for discriminating based on a health factor, and not be highly suspect in the method chosen to promote health or prevent disease.

(3) Are individuals who are eligible to participate given a chance to qualify at least once per year? (29 CFR 2590.702(f)(2)(iii))   Yes   No

(4) Is the reward available to all similarly situated individuals? Does the program offer a reasonable alternative standard? (29 CFR 2590.702(f)(2)(iv))   Yes   No

The wellness program rules require that the reward be available to all similarly situated individuals. A component of meeting this criterion is that the program must have a reasonable alternative standard (or waiver of the otherwise applicable standard) for obtaining the reward for any individual for whom, for that period:

o It is unreasonably difficult due to a medical condition to satisfy the otherwise applicable standard; OR

o It is medically inadvisable to attempt to satisfy the otherwise applicable standard.

It is permissible for the plan or issuer to seek verification, such as a statement from the individual's physician, that a health factor makes it unreasonably difficult or medically inadvisable for the individual to satisfy or attempt to satisfy the otherwise applicable standard.

(5) Does the plan disclose the availability of a reasonable alternative in all plan materials describing the program? (29 CFR 2590.702(f)(2)(v))   Yes   No

The plan or issuer must disclose the availability of a reasonable alternative standard *in all plan materials describing the program.* If plan materials merely mention that the program is available, without describing its terms, this disclosure is not required.

TIP: The disclosure does not have to say what the reasonable alternative standard is in advance. The plan can individually tailor the standard for each individual, on a case-by-case basis.

The following sample language can be used to satisfy this requirement: "If it is unreasonably difficult due to a medical condition for you to achieve the standards for the reward under this program, call us at [insert telephone number] and we will work with you to develop another way to qualify for the reward."

If you answered "Yes" to **ALL** of the 5 questions on wellness program criteria, there are no violations of the HIPAA wellness program rules.

If you answered "No" to **any** of the 5 questions on wellness program criteria, the plan has a wellness program compliance issue. Specifically,

Violation of the general benefit discrimination rule (29 CFR 2590.702(b)(2)(i))—If the wellness program varies benefits, including cost-sharing mechanisms (such as deductible, copayment, or coinsurance) based on whether an individual meets a standard related to a health factor *and* the program does not satisfy the requirements of 29 CFR 2590.702(f), the plan is impermissibly discriminating in benefits based on a health factor. The wellness program exception at 29 CFR 2590.702(b)(2)(ii) is not satisfied and the plan is in violation of 29 CFR 2590.702(b)(2)(i).

Violation of general premium discrimination rule (29 CFR 2590. 702(c)(1))—If the wellness program varies the amount of premium or contribution it requires similarly situated individuals to pay based on whether an individual meets a standard related to a health factor *and* the program does not satisfy the requirements of 29 CFR 2590.702(f), the plan is impermissibly discriminating in premiums based on a health factor. The wellness program exception at 29 CFR 2590.702(c)(3) is not satisfied and the plan is in violation of 29 CFR 2590.702(c)(1).

Additional compliance information regarding the other provisions in Part 7 of ERISA, including the HIPAA portability provisions and the rest of the HIPAA nondiscrimination provisions, is available on the Department's website at: http://www.dol.gov/ebsa/pdf/CAGAppA.pdf.

Questions concerning the information contained in this Bulletin may be directed to the Office of Health Plan Standards and Compliance Assistance at 202-693-8335.

Checklist for Planning Employee Health Risk Appraisal Implementation

Worksite: _____

Date: _____

HRA Objectives:

1)

2)

3)

HRA Administration

1. Is the HRA part of a planned, ongoing worksite health-promotion program?

❏ Yes ❏ No

Comment: _____

2. Has the worksite health or HRA planning team, including representatives from upper management, human resources, and the

legal department as appropriate, agreed on written objectives for conducting an HRA at this worksite?

❏ Yes ❏ No

Comment: _____

3. Has the worksite health or HRA planning team agreed on the HRA mode of administration, incentives (if used), type of feedback, and level of follow-up provided for participants?

❏ Yes ❏ No

Comment: _____

4. Are safeguards in place to ensure participant confidentiality, and is there a plan for communicating this to employees?

❏ Yes ❏ No

Comment: _____

5. Is the HRA target audience well defined?

❏ Yes ❏ No

Comment: _____

6. Has a communication plan been developed to promote the HRA and provide individual results to participants?

❏ Yes ❏ No

Comment: _____

7. Is there a plan in place for how HRA results will be used (e.g., provision of follow-up services, aggregate data analysis) for program planning?

❏ Yes ❏ No

Comment: _____

HRA Vendor and Tool

8. Is the HRA vendor experienced, quality-oriented, and responsive to your worksite's needs; have you verified with references?

❏ Yes   ❏ No

Comment: _____

9. Were key factors included in selecting the HRA tool: data security, desired data and report format, understandable feedback for participants, others specific to your needs?

❏ Yes   ❏ No

Comment: _____

Health Risk Assessment Personnel

10. Do you have adequately trained personnel for all stages of the health risk assessment: planning, implementation, follow-up?

❏ Yes   ❏ No

Comment: _____

11. If biometrics are included in the HRA, have you made provisions to ensure accurate measurements (e.g., blood pressure, weight) for these questions?

❏ Yes   ❏ No

Comment: _____

12. Do you have adequately trained personnel to assist employees with HRA interpretation, counseling, and/or referrals?

❏ Yes   ❏ No

Comment: _____

Source: Centers for Disease Control and Prevention Healthier Workforce Initiative (http://www.cdc.gov)

Appendix E

Sample Waiver and Release of Claims

(Reprinted (adapted) with permission of the American Psychological Association. For more information about the Psycologically Healthy Workplace Program, visit www.ohwa.org)
[Have your legal advisor review this form before use.]

I want to use the exercise room/fitness center subject to the conditions and statements set forth below. In return for permission to use the exercise room/fitness center, I agree to these conditions and statements. They are as follows:

1. I realize that exercise and the use of exercise equipment can result in injury or other adverse physiological effects.

2. I realize that the exercise room/fitness center does not have an attendant or supervisor.

3. I agree to use the exercise room/fitness center entirely at my own risk. I will not hold (name of company/organization), or any officer, employee, or agent of (name) responsible for injury or other adverse physiological effect, of whatever nature whatsoever, resulting from exercise, use of the exercise equipment, or the actions or conduct of others in the exercise room/fitness center.

4. I waive and release any and all causes of action, claims, demands, damages, and liability whatsoever that I or my representatives may have now or in the future against (name) or any officer, employee, or agent of (name), relating to exercise, use of the exercise equipment, or the actions or conduct of others in the exercise

room/fitness center. I or my representatives will not file a lawsuit or any other kind of complaint or action against (name) or any officer, employee, or agent of (name), concerning such causes of action, claims, demands, damages, and liabilities whatsoever.

_____
Signature
Name (please print)
Access Card Number
Date

Notes

All quotes that do not have citations are from interviews with the subjects, conducted by the author.

CHAPTER 1

1. Towers Perrin, *2008 Health Care Cost Survey*, 2008.
2. Don R. Powell, "How to Achieve an R.O.I. on Your Health Care Dollars," *Employee Benefits Journal* 27, no. 1 (2002): 24–27.
3. Congressional Budget Office, "Key Issues in Analyzing Major Health Insurance Proposals," December 2008. Summary.
4. Mercer and Kronos Incorporated, *The Total Financial Impact of Employee Absences,* Survey, October 2008.
5. CCH Inc., *Unscheduled Absence Survey,* 2007.
6. Ron Z. Goetzel, Stacey R. Long, Ronald J. Ozminkowski, Kevin Hawkins, Shaohung Wang, and Wendy Lynch, "Health, Absence, Disability, and Presenteeism Cost Estimates of Certain Physical and Mental Health Conditions Affecting U.S. Employers," *Journal of Occupational & Environmental Medicine* 46, no. 4 (April 2004): 398–412.
7. Steven G. Aldana, Roger L. Greenlaw, Audrey Salberg, Hans A. Diehl, Ray M. Merrill, Camille Thomas, and Seiga Ohmine, "The Behavioral and Clinical Effects of Therapeutic Lifestyle Change on Middle-aged Adults," *Centers for Disease Control and Prevention* 3, no. 1 (2006): A05.
8. Watson Wyatt, "Few Employers Addressing Workplace Stress, Watson Wyatt Surveys Find," *Press Release,* February 14, 2008.
9. D. W. Edington, "Emerging Research: A View from One Research Center," *American Journal of Health Promotion* 15, no. 5 (2001): 341–49.
10. Susan J. Wells, "Finding Wellness's Return on Investment," *HR Magazine,* June 2008: 74–84.
11. Troy Adams, "The ROI Calculator," *WELCOA's Absolute Advantage* 7, no. 5 (2008): 28–33.
12. Ron Z. Goetzel and Ronald J. Ozminkowski, *Annual Review of Public Health* 29 (April 2009): 303–23.

13. Union Pacific, "Raising Heart and Overall Health Awareness: Union Pacific Links Wellness Programs With Business and Medical Initiatives," *Press Release*, February 11, 2005.

14. WELCOA, "Union Pacific . . . On The Right Track," WELCOA Web site, Platinum Award 2001.

15. Union Pacific, WELCOA Well Workplace Platinum Award: Executive Summary, 2000.

CHAPTER 2

1. P. Hemp, "Presenteeism: At Work—But Out of It," *Harvard Business Review*, October 2004, 49–58, 155.

2. David Hunnicutt, "When It Comes from You . . . The Power of the CEO in Advancing a Wellness Initiative," *Absolute Advantage, WELCOA* 2008, 14.

3. Ibid.

4. Andrea Tortora, "Executive Health Programs All the Rage," *Business Courier of Cincinnati*, December 6, 2002, http://cincinnati.bizjournals.com/cincinnati/.

CHAPTER 3

1. David Hunnicutt, Jennifer Johnson, Angie Baldwin, Brittanie Leffelman, and Beth Hazen, *Building World Class Wellness Programs—Volume 1* (1999) "Crafting an Operating Plan," *Well Informed:1–4* 1, no. 5.

2. David Hunnicutt, Jennifer Johnson, Angie Deming, Beth Baadte, and Andrea Stephens, *Building World Class Wellness Programs—Volume 1* (1999) "Creating a Cohesive Wellness Team," *Well Informed:1–4* 1, no. 3.

3. Ibid.

4. WELCOA, *The Magic Numbers . . . Establishing Targets for Health Assessment Participation and the Percent of Employees at Low-Risk*, 2009.

5. Ibid.

6. The Health Project, *2006 C. Everett Koop National Award Winner: The USAA Take Care of Your Health Program*, C. Everett Koop National Health Awards, 2006.

CHAPTER 4

1. Coalition for the Advancement of Health Through Behavioral and Social Science Research, http://www.cossa.org/caht-bssr/caht-bssr.shtml.

2. C. L. Ogden, M. D. Carroll, M. A. McDowell, and K. M. Flegal, *Obesity Among Adults in the United States—No Change Since 2003–2004*, NCHS data brief no 1. (Hyattsville, MD: National Center for Health Statistics, 2007), http://www.cdc.gov/nchs/.

3. U.S. Department of Health and Human Services, *Prevention Makes Common Cents: Estimated Economic Costs of Obesity to U.S. Business*, (Washington, DC: U.S. Department of Health and Human Services, 2003), http://www.hhs.gov/.

4. "Walking Packs Huge Health Punch, Study Confirms," *Reuters Health*, December, 17, 2007, http://www.reutershealth.com/en/index.html.

5. *One Hundred Best Companies to Work for 2008 Fortune*, February 4, 2008, http://money.cnn.com/magazines/fortune/.

6. Bob Brady, "Wellness Programs: Do They Pay a Return on Investment?" *Business & Legal Reports,* March 28, 2006, http://www.blr.com/.

7. Craig Silverman, "Better Than Your Desk Mate Sweatin' to the Oldies," *Globe and Mail,* July 30, 2007, http://www.theglobeandmail.com/.

8. Rob Lever, *Treadmill Workstation Brings Exercise to Office, Slowly, Agence France Presse,* July 13, 2008, http://www.afp.com/afpcom/en.

9. Kelley M. Butler, "Benefits Leadership in Health Plans," *Employee Benefit News,* September 15, 2006: 42.

CHAPTER 5

1. National Business Group on Health & Watson Wyatt, *13th Annual National Business Group on Health/Watson Wyatt Report,* report, March, 2008. http://www.businessgrouphealth.org/.

2. Guardian Life Insurance Company of America, **Despite Perceived Effectiveness, Most Employees Who Participate in Wellness Programs Do Not Stay Committed,** survey, March 2008. http://www.guardianlife.com/.

3. Jack Mahoney, David Hom, *Total Value, Total Return: Seven Rules for Optimizing Employee Health Benefits for a Healthier and More Productive Workforce* (Philadelphia, PA: GlaxoSmithKline, 2006), http://www.gsk.com/.

4. Stephen G. Minter, "Providing an Incentive for Wellness," *Occupational Hazards,* October 4, 2005 http://ehstoday.com/.

5. Business & Legal Reports Inc., "Employer Uses Big, Sweet Carrot to Encourage Wellness," January 26, 2009 http://www.blr.com/.

6. Jennifer Brown, "Companies Rewarding Good Health With Gifts," *Denver Post,* January 26, 2009 http://www.denverpost.com/.

7. Wellness Program Management Advisor and Wellness Junction, *Wellness Managers' Use of Incentives for Program Participation Continues to Grow,* survey, May 11, 2007.

8. Gail Bensinger, "Corporate Wellness, Safeway Style," *San Francisco Chronicle,* January 4, 2009 http://www.sfgate.com/.

9. Karen Pallarito, "Employers Target Bad Habits for Insurance Coverages," *HealthDay News,* January 17, 2006 http://www.healthday.com/.

10. Knowledge@Wharton, the university's online business journal; Janice Bellace, a professor of legal studies and business ethics at The Wharton School of the University of Pennsylvania.

11. Milt Freudenheim, "Seeking Savings, Employers Help Smokers Quit," *New York Times,* October 26, 2007 http://www.nytimes.com/.

12. Stephenie Overman, "Wanted: Non-Smokers," *Staffing Management* 4, no. 1 (January–March 2008): 29–34.

13. Barbara Rose, "Employers Experiment with Tough Get-Healthy Regimes," *Chicago Tribune,* February 10, 2008 htttp://www.chicagotribune.com/.

14. U.S. Department of Labor Employee Benefits Security Administration, web site "FAQs About The HIPAA Nondiscrimination Requirements," http://www.dol.gov/ebsa/faqs/faq_hipaa_ND.html.

15. Stephenie Overman, "Lincoln Plating Benefits from Strategic Wellness Program," *Employee Benefit News,* October 2005. http://www.benefitnews.com/.

16. Ibid.

CHAPTER 6

1. Centers for Disease Control and Prevention Healthier Workforce Initiative, http://www.cdc.gov.

2. Ibid.

3. Leah Carlson Shephard, "Mandatory Health Screenings Reap Huge Rewards," *Employee Benefit News,* April 2006: 32.

CHAPTER 7

1. Elizabeth B. Krieger, "Finding Time Is Always a Challenge. It's Just Gotten Easier," *WebMD,* April 24, 2000, http://www.webmd.com/.

2. Nancy Hatch Woodward, "Exercise Options," *HR Magazine* 50, no. 6 (June 2005), www.shrm.org.

3. Medica, *The Health and Financial Benefits of Exercise,* Medica and Life Time Fitness study, 2007.

4. "Age-friendly Facilities: 99 Questions to Assess Your Center," International Council on Active Aging, http://www.icaa.cc.

5. The Health Project, *2006 C. Everett Koop National Award Winner, Motorola–Global Wellness Initiatives,* 2002.

6. Arnold M. Knightly, "A Healthy Harrah's," *Las Vegas Business Press,* September 7, 2007, http://www.lvbusinesspress.com/.

7. Watson Wyatt Worldwide and National Business Group on Health, *Dashboard for Success: How Best Performers Do It,* National Business Group on Health/Watson Wyatt survey, March, 2008.

8. McLean Robbins, "Employers Can See Guaranteed ROI from Onsite Health Clinics," *Employee Benefit News,* January 1, 2008, http://www.benefitnews.com/.

9. Susan J. Wells, "The Doctor Is In-House," *HR Magazine* 51, no. 4 (April 2006): 48–54.

10. Ibid.

11. Sanford Nowlin, "Toyota Med Center Provides It All," *Express-News,* November 23, 2008.

12. Ibid.

13. Julie Appleby, "Companies Step Up Wellness Efforts," *USA Today,* July 31, 2005, http://www.usatoday.com.

CHAPTER 8

1. R.C. Kessler, H.S. Akiskal, M. Ames, H. Birnbaum, P. A. Greenberg, M. Robert, R. Jin, K. R. Merikangas, G. E. Simon, and P. S. Wang, "Prevalence and Effects of Mood Disorders on Work Performance in a Nationally Representative Sample of U.S. Workers," *American Journal of Psychiatry* 163 (2006): 1561–68.

2. American Psychological Association, *Stress Survey: Stress a Major Health Problem in the U.S.,* 2007, http://www.apa.org/.

3. Madison Park, "Study: 8 out of 10 Americans Stressed Because of Economy," CNN Web site, December 9, 2008, http://www.cnn.com/.

4. P. S. Wang, G. E. Simon, J. Avorn, F. Azocar, E. J. Ludman, J. McCulloch, M. Z. Petukhova, and R. C. Kessler, "Telephone Screening, Outreach and Care Management for Depressed Workers and Impact on Clinical and Work Productivity Outcomes, a Randomized Controlled Trial," *Journal of the American Medical Association* 298, no. 12 (September 26, 2007): 1401–11.

5. Ellen Galinsky, James T. Bond, and Kelly Sakai, *2008 National Study of Employers*, Families and Work Institute, New York, May 2008, http://www.familiesandwork.org/.

6. M. Attridge, "Personal and Work Outcomes of Employee Assistance Services" (presented at the American Psychological Association Annual Meeting, San Francisco, CA, August 2001).

7. Editorial Staff, "Workplace Stress Research Promotes Benefits," Employee Benefit News, February 17, 2009, http://www.benefitnews.com/.

8. U.S. Department of Labor, Bureau of Labor Statistics, *Job Openings and Labor Turnover Survey (JOLT)*, http://www.bls.gov/.

9. American Psychological Association, *APA Announces 2008 Psychologically Healthy Workplace Award Winners*, March 25, 2008, http://www.apa.org/.

10. Kelly K. Spors, "Top Small Workplaces 2007," *Wall Street Journal*, October 1, 2007, www.wallstreetjournal.com.

11. Howard H. Goldman, *New England Journal of Medicine* 354, no. 13 (March 30, 2006): 1378–86.

CHAPTER 9

1. "Workforce Health-Management Programs Bring Bottom-Line Benefits," *Aegis Thought Paper* 1, no.1 (2009).

2. Frank Diamond, "Employers Roll Up Their Sleeves," *Managed Care*, August 2007, http://www.managedcaremag.com/.

3. PricewaterhouseCooper's Health Research Institute, *What Employers Want from Health Insurers—Now*, http://www.pwc.com/.

4. America's Health Insurance Plans, *Innovations in Prevention, Wellness and Risk Reduction Innovations in Prevention, Wellness and Risk Reduction*, 2008, http://www.ahip.org/.

5. Frank Diamond, "Employers Roll Up Their Sleeves," *Managed Care*, August 2007, http://www.managedcaremag.com/.

6. "Accelerating the Adoption of Preventive Health Services Building New Partnerships and Community Commitment" (convened by The National Institute for Health Care Management [NIHCM] Research and Educational Foundation, 2003), http://www.nihcm.org.

7. Ibid.

8. Martin Sipkoff, "Employers' Stock in Wellness Rises with No End in Sight," *Managed Care*, July 2006, http://www.managedcaremag.com/.

9. Stephen Miller, "CDHP Enrollees More Health- and Cost-Conscious," SHRM Online, October 20, 2008, http://www.shrm.org.

10. Jay Greene, America's Health Insurance Plans, "Guiding the Way to Wellness: Plans Are Increasingly Relying on Health Coaches as Part of the Team or

Approach That Encourages Patients to Adopt Healthy Habits," July/August 2007, http://www.ahip.org.

11. America's Health Insurance Plans, "Innovations in Prevention, Wellness and Risk Reduction Innovations in Prevention, Wellness and Risk Reduction," 2008. http://www.ahip.org.

CHAPTER 10

1. Sarah Kornblet, Joy Prittsa, Melissa Goldstein, Tom Perez, and Sara Rosenbaum, *Patient Race and Ethnicity Data and Quality Reporting; A Legal 'Roadmap' to Transparency*, George Washington University School of Public Health & Health Services, Department of Health Policy, Policy Brief 4, March 2008.

2. Patty Kujawa, "Tackling Health Problems by Addressing Racial Disparities," Workforce Management, May 2008, http://www.workforce.com/.

3. CompPsych Corp., *New Study Shows Older Workers Are Healthiest, Workers in 30s Most at Risk*, August 25, 2008.

4. Kristen B. Frasch, "Leading Healthier Lives," *Human Resource Executive*, September 25, 2008.

5. "Different Generations Seek Health Care Information Differently, Study Finds," *Nashville Business Journal*, June 12, 2008, http://www.nashville.bizjournals.com/.

6. "Wellness Programs and Your Aging Workforce," *The Life Care Connection* 36, quarter 2 (2005), http://www.lifecareconnections.com.

7. Research Agenda for Psychosocial and Behavioral Factors in Women's Health, 1996.

8. American Psychological Association briefing sheet, American Psychological Association, Washington, D.C., http://www.apa.org/.

9. "Survey Finds More Women Call Employee Assistance Programs," HR.com, August 3, 2007, http://www.hr.com/.

10. Leah Carlson Shepherd, "Minority Report," *Employee Benefit News*, March 24, 2009.

11. "Hispanics Have Unique Cancer 'Profile'," *HealthDay News*, September 13, 2006.

12. Henry G. Cisneros, ed., with John Rosales, *Latinos and the Nation's Future* (Houston, TX: Arte Publico Press, 2009).

13. Bob Calandra, "Medical Mistrust," *Human Resource Executive*, March 10, 2009.

14. National Committee for Quality Assurance, "Recognizing Innovation in Multicultural Health Care Award," 2008.

15. Eileen Elias, "Shaping the Future of Disability Research" (International Committee on Disability Research ISE Interagency Subcommittee on Employment summit, June 2008).

16. Stephen Miller, "Wellness: Program Reaps Cost Savings for Unionized Workforce," SHRM Online Compensation & Benefits Focus Area, April 1, 2006, http://www.shrm.org.

17. Buck Consultants, *WORKING WELL: A Global Survey of Health Promotion and Workplace Wellness Strategies*, October 9, 2008.

18. Stephenie Overman, "Wellness Philosophy May Be Global, but Programs Are Localized," SHRM Online, http://www.shrm.org.

19. Susan Gurevitz, "Building a Global Wellness Imitative," *HR Executive,* June 8, 2005.

20. Stephenie Overman, "Wellness Philosophy May Be Global, but Programs Are Localized," SHRM Online, http://www.shrm.org.

21. Susan Gurevitz, "Building a Global Wellness Imitative," *HR Executive,* June 8, 2005.

22. *How to Set Up a Wellness Plan,* (: How-To Guide The Wall Street Journal/ Small Business, http://guides.wsj.com/small-business/.

23. David Hunnicutt, "The Art of Implementing a Great Workplace Wellness Program in a Small Business Setting," *Absolute Advantage* WELCOA, 2008, 7(1), 3–9.

Resources

ORGANIZATIONS

Alliance for Wellness ROI Inc.: http://www.roiwellness.org

American Cancer Society: http://www.cancer.org

American Diabetes Association: http://www.diabetes.org

American Dietetic Association: http://www.eatright.org

American Heart Association: http://www.americanheart.org

American Hospital Association: http://www.aha.org

American Institute for Preventative Medicine: http://www.healthylife.com/

American Lung Association: http://www.lungusa.org/

American Psychological Association: http://www.apa.org/

Center for the Advancement of Health: http://www.cfah.org

Centers for Disease Control and Prevention: http://www.cdc.gov/

Employee Assistance Professionals Association: http://www.eapassn.org

Employee Assistance Society of North America: http://www.easna.org/home.asp

The Health Project: http://www.emory.edu/healthproject/

Healthy People 2010: http://www.healthypeople.gov

Health Enhancement Research Organization (HERO): http://www.the-hero.org/

Institute for Health and Productivity: http://www.ihpm.org

Mental Health America: http://www.nmha.org/

National Business Group on Health: http://www.businessgrouphealth.org

National Cancer Institute: http://www.cancer.gov/

National Institute of Mental Health: http://www.nimh.nih.gov/, http://www.nimh.nih.gov/healthinformation/depressionmenu.cfm

National Wellness Institute: http://www.nationalwellness.org/

National Workrights Institute: http://www.workrights.org/

Nicotine Anonymous: http://www.nicotine-anonymous.org/

Office of Minority Health: http://www.omhrc.gov

Overeaters Anonymous: http://www.oa.org

Partnership for Prevention: http://www.prevent.org/

Small Business Wellness Initiative: http://www.sbwi.org

Smokefree.gov

Society for Human Resource Management: http://www.shrm.org

University of Michigan Worker Health Program: http://www.ilir.umich.edu/well ness/comprehensiveprogram.html

Wellness Council of Americas (WELCOA): http://www.welcoa.org/

Wellness Junction: http://www.wellnessjunction.com/

PUBLICATIONS

American Journal of Health Behavior: http://www.kittle.siu.edu/ajhb/

American Journal of Health Promotion: http://www.healthpromotionjournal.com/

American Journal of Preventive Medicine: http://www.elsevier.com/locate/amepre

Employee Benefit News: http://www.benefitnews.com/

Health & Fitness Journal (American College of Sports Medicine): http://www. acsm.org

Journal of the American Medical Association (JAMA): http://jama.ama-assn.org/

Journal of Occupational & Environmental Medicine: http://www.acoem.org/joem.aspx

Journal of Occupational Health Psychology: http://www.apa.org/journals/ocp/

Index

About the Author

STEPHENIE OVERMAN has written extensively about health care and wellness for publications including *HR Magazine, Staffing Management Magazine, Employee Benefit News, The Los Angeles Business Journal,* and *Physicians Financial News.* A former senior writer for the Society for Human Resource Management's *HR Magazine,* she is editor of the Society's *Staffing Management* magazine.